YOU'LL NEVER GUESS WHAT HE DID THEN . . .

Whether your hot new date turns out to be the local flasher, or your earring repairs while driving to meet the man of your dreams leave you with your hand superglued to the gearstick, dating is fraught with the potential for triumph . . . and disaster.

The hilarious episodes gathered here may make you cringe, hit your head against the wall or hide under the table, but there's no doubt that most of all they will make you laugh – because there is nothing to beat a date from hell that has never quite happened to you!

DATES FROM HELL

Maryon Tysoe's articles on 'Dates from Hell' in *New Woman* and the *Daily Express* and a competition in *Time Out* led to a flood of letters describing astonishingly hellish dates. The funniest are here.

Also by Maryon Tysoe:

All This and Work Too
Love Isn't Quite Enough

Dates from Hell

Edited by
Maryon Tysoe

HEADLINE

First published in 1994 by
HEADLINE BOOK PUBLISHING

10 9 8 7 6 5 4 3 2 1

ISBN 0 7472 4572 X

Typeset by Avon Dataset Ltd., Bidford-on-Avon

Printed and bound in Great Britain by
Cox & Wyman Ltd, Reading, Berks.

HEADLINE BOOK PUBLISHING
A division of Hodder Headline PLC
338 Euston Road
London NW1 3BH

Acknowledgements

My editor, Anna Powell, deserves my sincere thanks for commissioning this book and thus giving me the chance to have some fun. But even fun can be a hell of a strenuous business, so I'd also like to thank her and my agent, Vivien Green, for mopping my brow whenever I and my word processor overheated.

My most grateful thanks of all are due, of course, to those without whom there would be no book: to the readers of *New Woman*, the *Daily Express* and *Time Out* who sent me their stories in response to my articles and competitions; and to my friends and friends of friends who told me their tales (and who, naturally, I shall never name . . . !).

Contents

Editor's Note

To protect the innocent – and the guilty – *all names have been changed*, both of the contributors and of everyone mentioned in their stories. Many details have been deleted or altered, too (for example, of physical appearance, possessions and geographical location). So if, by any extremely remote chance, anyone reading this recognizes themselves as the star of a Date – fear not. No one else will ever know it was you if you don't choose to tell!

1
'I couldn't believe it':
Disappointment 1

I'd fancied James for ages when we'd worked for the same company. I was eighteen and he about thirty-four. I knew he was engaged to another girl and seeing someone else on the side – obviously a bit of a rogue, but very sexy with it.

A couple of years later, when I'd moved to a job in London and he had set up his own business, he rang me out of the blue and suggested we go out to dinner. I was flabbergasted and flattered, after all that time.

I should have known what he was like, particularly when he put his arm round me and tried to kiss me before we'd even left my flat!

I was incredibly nervous, particularly as my flatmates had been really winding me up about my hunky date. We walked to a local restaurant and I'm afraid that nerves got the better of me and I downed rather a lot of wine with my meal.

It was getting more and more obvious that James was a real smoothie, not my type at all. I couldn't believe I'd not twigged before – and I really couldn't see what he saw in me. By the time the sweet arrived he was talking saucy and I was plastered. The loveable rogue was fast turning into a creep.

Eventually I got so fed up with his smarminess that

I went to the loo for a breather. The open window there gave me an idea. In my drunken state I hoisted myself on to the washbasin and got my head and shoulders through the window, ready to make an escape and run home. Unfortunately, I hadn't counted on my shoulder-bag getting caught on the window catch. I was well and truly wedged halfway out of the window and unable to get back in or out. As if that wasn't bad enough, I developed the worst case of hiccups I've ever had and could feel my face getting hotter and hotter.

After what seemed like an age, another diner came into the toilets and stood transfixed by my bum hanging in what must have seemed like mid-air. After a drunken explanation, she helped pull me back through the window on to the basin, where I caught the heel of my shoe which promptly snapped off with a loud click.

By this time I'd been in the toilets about half an hour and when, very red-faced, I returned to James at the table he just said, 'And I thought you'd got fed up with me and escaped out the window!'

I choked down a laugh and said there'd been a queue.

Not very realistic when there were only four other people in the restaurant.

But this was not the end.

I decided to make the best of it and James suggested a stroll to walk off the meal. Ten minutes later, in a surprised voice, he said 'Oh fancy, that's my hotel, why don't we go in for a nightcap?'

Original, or what?

Before I knew what was happening, and still rather inebriated but trying to act sober, I was dragged hobbling into the foyer and whisked into a waiting lift.

In what seemed like one fell swoop we were in his bedroom.

By this time I just wanted out. So I turned on the TV and sat on the edge of the bed avidly watching some late-night quiz programme.

Terribly terribly avidly.

After about ten minutes I heard cheesed-off coughing noises and restless movements. I found the courage to say I was tired and needed my bed.

He weakly suggested his. I declined.

Needless to say I never heard from my worst-date-ever again. The relief was enormous.

Sarah N., 29, personal assistant

🐛🐛🐛

It was the first time I'd gone away for the weekend with my new boyfriend. He drove us to a little hotel in the country. I began to sense that perhaps he wasn't quite . . .

On our return, my best friend asked me how it went. 'Well,' I said, womanfully, 'it was sort of all right.'

Significant pause while I debated whether or not I could bring myself to come clean.

'But when we got back, he pulled out his calculator. He worked out my share of the petrol and added in a percentage for depreciation on the car.'

Janet B., 32, local council officer

৵৵৵

I'd got this holiday job working in the lingerie department of a big department store. I was studying physics at college and needed the money. Men were always coming in and out, buying glorious underwear for their wives and girlfriends – and mistresses.

One day, this real hunk came in, wanting something pretty for his sister. We got talking, and he asked me for a drink at the local wine bar after work.

Why not? I thought. Seems bright and down to earth, things I like in a man. And muscly.

We wedged ourselves in at a corner table among the hordes recovering from the stresses of having to work and ordered a bottle of house plonk.

We chatted about his job – a trainee solicitor, which sounded promising. I told him about my course and the excitements of scientific research. We exchanged horror stories about our bank managers, and agreed that they all grow hairs on their palms at the time of the full moon.

It was all going swimmingly. Then, over the second bottle, he suddenly leaned towards me, gazed into my eyes and said 'I bet you're a Sagittarius.'

Uh oh.

Telling him I think astrology is a load of old bollocks might not be the wisest move here, I thought. Anyway, lots of people believe in astrology. Don't be so judgmental, for heaven's sake.

'No, actually, I'm Aries,' I said.

'Aries is glorious,' he said. 'I'm Gemini. We're made

for each other, I just know we are. Our celestial spirits will blend for all eternity. I can see your aura – it throbs and glows, gold like your eyes. You have an old soul. I'm going for a session of chakra meditation at a Zen monastery up north next weekend. Would you . . .'

'Er no, thanks,' I said. 'I have to go and see my brother and his wife. They're great,' I went on, in a desperate attempt to turn the conversation into non-cosmic channels. 'How many siblings have you got?'

'None,' he said, 'I'm an only child.'

'But you were buying a silk petticoat for your sister . . .'

'Oh,' he said, blushing, 'that was for me.'

Jane R., 24, teacher

🍀🍀🍀

Handsome businessman, 29, would like to meet modern girl.

Well, I thought, given the rather large gap in my love life, he might be worth a try.

It's a cold Friday night. I've dressed to fit the requirements of what I'm hoping will be a distinguished-looking, immaculately dressed and (fingers doubly crossed) filthy rich gentleman. 'Oh God,' I mutter to myself, 'what am I doing?'

I could hear my mother recoil on the phone as I'd tried to tell her about her possible future son-in-law. She wasn't listening. Was I that desperate? Did I want

5

to end up murdered in a back street? No, actually – but I wouldn't mind a free meal and a taxi home, Mother.

So with my bag clutched close to my trembling heart, I cross the street to meet either my destiny or my doom.

A tall, dark and vaguely handsomeish bloke approaches me with a smile. He's in jeans and I'm wearing a long black skirt complete with thigh-high split.

Too late to worry.

'Hello Jo,' he says. 'I'm Richard. How are you?' (Wishing, if you must know, that my periodic spurts of self-confidence wouldn't take such a hold on my otherwise shy and retiring personality. I could be quietly at home now. With my crochet.)

We make our way to a public house and I discover that Richard has quite a creative way with words. 'Businessman' to me conjures images of Turnbull and Asser ties, cellnet phones and L-reg company cars.

Well, I got the last bit right. Except Richard doesn't own a car – he sells them. One of them is to be my lift home later, he says, pointing it out a bit further up the road. Scanning for the high-performance Jag, I spot the one he means. The Lada with the ever-so-slightly crumpled boot.

I am so nervous I feel drunk before my first vodka. I keep tripping over words to hurry the conversation along so that the evening will draw to a close swiftly. No joy – he seems intent on dwelling, mysteriously, on my convent school past. I decide to ask him why he placed an advertisement in a lonely hearts column.

'Hey,' he drawls. 'I'm a busy man. I haven't the time

to meet the ladies on a social basis. Besides,' he lowers his voice, 'to tell you the truth, I'm a guy. A red-hot-blooded guy with red-hot needs.'

Now I see what he meant by 'modern girl'.

What kind of partner was he hoping to find, I venture tentatively.

'I like women who know about the good things in life. I like them to be petite, with long blonde hair, big, er, you know, and have loads of money.' So, why did you answer my letter which clearly stated that I was a little on the voluptuous side, with a mass of brown curly hair and that I was definitely a student of the poorest sort?

'Well your letter made me laugh and I thought, Richard, why not? Who knows where the evening will end? My taste buds could be reawakened – know what I mean?'

I certainly do and pray for a miracle. Jesus doesn't appear and neither do any ex-boyfriends. Before I can say 'I've changed my mind, I'm going to be a nun,' I find myself slouched in the front seat of the Lada – perfumed with a striking whiff of cat fluids – on the way home.

Having made it quite clear that I am a very old-fashioned girl indeed – no, I don't even kiss cheeks on the first date – I shut the front door firmly in his face.

Perhaps mothers are always right. I phone mine to let her know that I'm not a dead body lying in a gutter – and I definitely won't be leaving my crochet for quite some time.

Jo F., 21, student

ༀ-ༀ-ༀ

Don used to come into the office where I worked once or twice a week, and we always used to have a laugh and a chat. When he asked me out for a Chinese meal, I was delighted, and spent an ill-afforded fortune on a new skirt and blouse. Chinese restaurants can be quite swanky.

He picked me up in an estate car with a child seat in the back, saying the car was his brother's and that his own was in for repair following an accident. He'd certainly mentioned having a bump in the car the previous week.

I was looking forward to dinner in a stylish restaurant. Suddenly, I caught sight of something else in the back seat. Our Chinese meal. In a take-away carrier bag.

We went to his house, and had the meal and a bottle of cheap wine. He told me that his wife had left him, taking the children. I did feel sorry for him. The house didn't feel quite as bachelor-like as I expected, but he said he hadn't got the heart to erase all traces of them from the house.

Don did, however, have the heart to make a pass, and was getting quite amorous when the phone rang. It was his wife, who had indeed left him. For a few days, to stay with her mother.

Pat G., 37, window dresser

ༀ-ༀ-ༀ

I met Pete one hot August Bank Holiday weekend. We were camping at a pop festival and spent the last night sleeping out under the stars together. He was so romantic and I managed to convince myself that this was IT. A few weeks later, I invited him to come and stay with my family.

I spent the intervening weeks convincing all my friends that Pete was a demi-god, the epitome of handsome good taste and spine-tingling sensuality. Consequently, a whole group of us arranged to meet up at the local bowling alley upon his arrival, so that I could show him off to everybody.

Things started to go wrong as soon as he got off the coach. To my horror he was wearing a 'Teenage Mutant Ninja Turtles' T-shirt, while tied around his waist was a holey lilac jumper which had been hand-knitted by his granny. It was hard to decide which item of clothing was more embarrassing. He ignored my heavy hints about the 'nice men's jackets' as we took a short cut through a chain store. Instead he bragged about his skills with a ball and skittles all the way to the leisure centre.

Well, I'm no bowling expert, but I certainly know that my score of 127 was quite reasonable, whereas his total of 29 was abysmal. My friends made various snide remarks about me mistaking my imagination for my memory when describing my new man, and promptly left me to fend for myself. By this stage all I could think was 'ground', 'open up', 'swallow'.

To cut a long story short, the weekend didn't improve. Pete calmly helped himself to food from our kitchen cupboards and then refused to eat the meals my mother had cooked. He wore the same clothes for the next two days (I've got the photos to prove it), causing an outbreak of Ninja Turtle jokes in our household. He also spent most of his time sitting in the spare room reading all the back issues of *Viz* magazine which he'd brought with him.

The final straw came as I accompanied him to the bus station for his journey home. I plucked up the courage to express my displeasure at his behaviour over the previous forty-eight hours, to which he replied, 'Well if you don't want me, I've got plenty of others like you dotted around the country.' And with that he boarded the coach and was never seen again.

I was only fifteen when this catalogue of disasters occurred, but the memory still haunts me. The experience didn't quite put me off men for life, but it was a close thing . . .

Emma D., 18, economics student

🐾🐾🐾

I was eighteen, and had just split up with my boyfriend of a few months. He had been a real weirdo and also an alcoholic, so I was pleased when one of his friends asked me out for a drink. Here was someone relatively normal!

Anyway, we had a very pleasant evening and got on really well. Brian was much older than me (he was thirty) but I had found that boys my own age were a bit immature. Anyway, at the end of the evening he asked me if I wanted to come back to his flat for a coffee, so I went along.

When we arrived, he suggested that I made the coffee while he went to get something he wanted to show me. After about fifteen minutes he reappeared in the kitchen. He'd clearly changed into something more comfortable.

A bra, knickers, stockings and suspenders, all in an attractive pale pink.

I shot out of the door, trying desperately not to laugh. Had I got a 'Weirdos welcome' sign on my forehead, or what?

Julie C., 25, student

🌷🌷🌷

Paul and I met at a Christmas party, held at the hospital where I'd been getting some work experience as part of my biology degree. What had drawn me towards him was his incredible deep blue eyes and his rather peculiar – to say the least – sense of dress. I mean, picture an alternating purple and white knitted jumper with yellow trousers. Anyway, the way I saw it, he had a lot of long-term possibilities. I still don't know what those possibilities were, but at the time, if Kevin Costner had strolled past naked I wouldn't have batted an eyelid. I reckoned a complete change of wardrobe, a good haircut and a new brand of face cream could do wonders for his potential to father my children. (I was feeling in rather a maternal mood.)

11

It must have been fate, because the next thing I knew he was strolling right towards me. 'Hey, my name's Paul, but my friends call me fartface. I'm a Virgo with Libra rising, I'm the only child in my family, I have a cat and a goldfish called Derek and before you ask, my little sweetpea, I'm single, available and great in bed!'

Well, the main question in my mind was 'Is he fertile?' but I thought I should restrain myself before relying on first impressions. 'Hey, my name's Sita,' I replied. After intense interrogation I discovered he was a volunteer at the hospital.

The party was a bit dead so we decided to go for a curry. It was weird, it was as if we'd known each other for ages. I found myself more and more attracted towards him, and all night we talked about each other's fantasies. But he did do something a bit over the top while we were ordering our meal – he insisted that all the plates, spoons and glasses we used should be thoroughly and repeatedly cleaned. At the time I thought 'Well, Mum, if you were here you'd be impressed!' The night ahead looked very promising. That night I went back to his place and had the most incredible sex ever.

The following morning I woke up wondering what our children would look like.

Suddenly, I felt a chill, so I got out of bed with the quilt wrapped around my body. Much to my surprise, every window and door in the house was open. 'Can't you smell it?' he yelled.

'Have you done a fart?' I said. 'Oh, so that's why your friends call you fartface?'

'Can't you smell the blood of dead bodies? I have to get rid of the smell!' he screamed.

So, this is what hospital work does to you.

'I've just got to see my careers adviser,' I gasped, and ran.

Sita B., 20, biology student

🐾🐾🐾

OK! So I'm a snob! What's more I'm a middle-aged, single snob, so when Jim started to follow me around, and call me three or four times a day, I was not even flattered.

His conversation was peppered with double negatives; his accent broad, sometimes unintelligible. But he was always clean and smartly, though casually, dressed.

Gradually (very gradually) he started to get through to me. His sense of humour, his tenacity, and most of all his earthy physical attraction finally persuaded me to agree to a date.

He made reservations at a very good restaurant in the country, and called for me on the dot of eight p.m. He looked stunning, told me I did too, etc. etc. I began to wonder why I hadn't seen behind the 'rough exterior' long before.

Well ... The dinner went well, food good, an attentive escort. I had relaxed and begun to enjoy myself when suddenly he sneezed, took the beautiful snowy white damask serviette off his knee, and –

blew his nose loud and long into it.

He then carefully screwed it up and put it back on the table in front of my plate.

From now on I think I will go by first impressions.

Claire J., 58, sales negotiator

🐛🐛🐛

Have you ever heard that little voice in your head screaming 'No! Say no!' but when you open your mouth 'Oh, yes, a film would be nice – Saturday then?' flows out instead? Exactly the dilemma I found myself in, and all because somewhere in the optimistic eternal search for 'man', the connection between brain and mouth had been severed.

To any normal human being, the words 'I don't like horror films' would surely convey some sort of message. But my new acquaintance couldn't have been either normal or human . . .

I had barely settled down with my popcorn before the first segment of intestine flashed on to the screen.

So, I thought, this is Mr Sensitive's special selection, is it?

The film really was nothing but violence, blood and gore. I spent the duration inspecting the walls, my handbag and my coat – in fact anything but the screen. For variety I occasionally shoved my fingers, complete with bits of popcorn, in my ears to block out the screams.

He did try to hold my hand, but the cold and clammy

appendage just added to the gruesome atmosphere. I pulled away.

An arm crept around my shoulders. I bit back a shriek.

Then we both sat perfectly still, him enthralled by the film, me not wanting to move in case he tried to get closer.

Eventually the film ended (hooray!) and I drove him home. I hesitated but accepted the offer of a cup of tea – it couldn't surely get any worse.

As I entered the house I noticed, in the downstairs cloakroom, snapshots of him with various women.

A 'conquests' board.

How could I escape and how soon?

I quickly started to mentally fill in each day of my diary just in case another invitation was in the offing.

While the tea brewed, he went into the dining-room to put on some music. I followed, and suddenly had to bite my lip hard to stop myself from giggling.

There we were, the three of us. Me, him, and a garden gnome. This was proudly positioned, centre place on the dining-room table. I just had to ask, I knew I shouldn't but I had to . . . 'Stupid question,' I started, 'but why do you have a gnome on the table?'

He looked at me in total disbelief, as if it was the most natural thing in the world and I must have been on Mars for the last decade. 'He was a present. Besides, he would get cold outside.'

Josie G., 28, graphic designer

❧❧❧

After being on my own for a year, I decided to answer three or four personal ads. I thought that I was being selective, looking for words like 'intelligent' and 'witty'. But I soon discovered that male advertisers seem to use these terms very loosely when applying them to themselves – they obviously don't base it on any concrete evidence. It must have just been a hunch or something.

Anyway, I arranged to meet this chap one morning outside a city pub. When he was ten minutes late I should have begun to suspect, and on glancing round I noticed a man across the street looking ill at ease and shifting from foot to foot. I toyed with the idea then of walking away, because I had the vague sensation that he had been watching me.

However, a temporary loss of sanity kept me there for another ten minutes. Sure enough, this awkward, fumbling person finally crossed the road and stood a few yards away from me. I couldn't contain myself any longer without bursting out laughing, so I turned and said his name as a question. He stumbled and mumbled an affirmative.

With a swift glance at my watch, mentally promising myself a sharp exit after ten minutes, and thinking, It can't be that bad, can it? we entered the pub. How wrong I was.

Over my coffee I learnt that he worked for a butcher, and was particularly interested in chickens. He quoted simply *fascinating* facts and figures about the UK's turnover in chickens, chicken-killing techniques, chickens in sickness and in health.

It was then that I made my big mistake. I told him I

16

was a psychiatric nurse, and I thought I noticed a gleam in his eye. He then unfolded the sorry tale of how his last girlfriend had stood him up a week before their wedding. I didn't particularly want to pursue the 'counselling session' role that was being thrust upon me. But his next revelation had me feeling surreptitiously for my bag and keys and seeing what obstacles there were between me and the door.

Feeling jilted, hurt, etc., by his girlfriend's actions, he explained, he thought of how to get back at her. At the time, he was a long-distance lorry driver. One day he drove to her town, knowing where she'd be. When she was in sight, he drove towards her, 'putting my foot down, half hoping she'd run, half hoping she wouldn't'. When the poor woman had to run literally for her life he felt, he said, a sense of justice and that he had 'shown her what for'.

'What did I think of that?' he asked.

What did I think of psychopathic attempts to run down his ex-girlfriend with an articulated lorry?

Suddenly unable to find my voice, I gesticulated that I would have to go as I was late for work.

'I can see you're impressed,' he said.

Irene N., 26, psychiatric staff nurse

❦❦❦

Several years ago I changed jobs, which meant relocating to a new area, away from all my friends and colleagues. Being single as well at the time, it meant I was feeling rather lonely and cut off while I adjusted to my new life.

However, a couple of weeks into the new job I was asked out for a drink by the manager of a particular company my firm used. I was delighted, as this guy was very good-looking and seemed 'my kind of man'.

My initial thoughts were only enhanced on our first date, a drink in the local pub after work. We seemed to have a lot in common: similar tastes in films, books, music and so on. So I had no hesitation in accepting an invitation to his place for supper that coming weekend.

The weekend arrived, and I took extra special care in making sure I looked absolutely perfect for my second date.

My first surprise of the evening was my date's house – for a good-looking hunk of a guy he did seem to like pink rather a lot. I brushed it off, thinking that perhaps he'd only just moved in recently, and would be redecorating.

We enjoyed a wonderful meal together, and I was invited to go and relax in the living-room while he made some coffee. As I waited I couldn't resist browsing through his rather large video collection; but was horrified to find they were *all* porn movies. He's a bit kinky then, I thought, and was quite embarrassed that they were all on such visible display.

Anyway, we settled down with our coffee and listened to some music. I found myself feeling very attracted to him. After all, it had been a long while since I had been in the company of a man.

Our kissing and cuddling soon heated up and he suggested we went upstairs. Great, I thought, this is just what I need. My date suggested I went up first while he fixed a couple of drinks and 'got himself ready'. Ready for what, I pondered, but upstairs I went.

His bedroom was full of photos of women. What a show-off, I thought, but went over to have a closer look. That's funny, I giggled, they all look a bit like him, perhaps they're his sister. Then it dawned on me.

They *were* him.

I then turned around to view the rest of his room, only to see it filled with leather masks, whips, and a pair of handcuffs casually hung on the bedpost.

'Oh, my goodness,' I cried, and began to panic. I knew I had to get out quick. This was not my cup of tea!

I heard him shout that he wouldn't be long, he was just finishing getting ready. I decided I didn't want to find out what he was getting ready for, and hurriedly shoved all his pillows under the covers so it would look like I was in bed. I even threw my jacket down by the door, so he would think I'd got undressed.

But how to escape?

I ran into the next bedroom, opened the window and climbed out on to the top of the garage. Risking life and limb I scrambled down, ripping my expensive silk shirt and ruining my shoes in the process. I reached the safety of my car in seconds.

I could hear him calling my name as I drove off. Once safely on the motorway, I began to laugh as I imagined his face when he realized I'd gone.

The next few times I saw him at work, I couldn't look him in the eye. He was obviously embarrassed too. But then I thought I'd have a lot more to tell about him than he would of me, and decided to pluck up the courage to ask for my jacket back. I enclosed this request, in writing, with some work he was doing for my company.

The next day I received a reply. 'Hope you don't mind, but I'm going to keep the jacket. It goes so well with one of my new dresses.'

Debbie F., 27, market researcher

🐸🐸🐸

On our second date I invited the handsome Australian to my place for a slap-up dinner. I was very eager to impress, so I made a rare appearance in the kitchen and spent the best part of two hours cooking up a lavish dish.

Dish prepared, lights dimmed and music playing softly in the background, I set my creation in front of him and took my seat opposite.

He looked at his plate with appreciation, opened his mouth to speak and then sneezed so hard over the table that his petit pois came rolling off his plate towards me.

Absolutely staggered, I stared aghast at the remains of his dinner, and then at mine which had also been showered. He too stared at the scattered food, saw the stony expression on my face and then burst into fits of laughter. He tried to apologize but then laughed so hard that the tears ran down his face.

Frostily, I cleared the table while he clutched his sides.

So it's back to restaurants for me. And people familiar with the concept of a handkerchief.

Sarah J., 23, civil servant

❧❧❧

I'd just split from my boyfriend and, at thirty-five, found myself reeling from dates with mostly younger men; they were so inconsiderate, lacking in style, no idea of how to treat a woman.

Jenny, my best friend, had been single for a while and warned me of what to expect of the single life: lots of younger men keen to boast about their older conquests; and terrible disappointment when they themselves don't live up to your expectations. But on the bright side, there were the parties.

I agreed immediately when she suggested we go to a Revival Dance that Friday. So we found ourselves in the local community centre, surrounded by a mixed crowd of happy socializers of all ages.

I had loved parties and dances of any kind in my teens and twenties, but settling into my long-term relationship with Gordon had ended all that and replaced it with TV and cooking. That had not been bad, but the lights of the dance-hall brought back memories of carefree days.

We headed for the bar and our customary orange juice, which I sipped while Jenny rushed over to say hello to a friend she'd spotted. Left alone, my thoughts turned to Gordon. But, determined not to spend the evening pining over him, I decided to follow Jenny. I turned only to find someone tall and in the way. On striding confidently forward, I splashed orange juice over his jacket. We stood face to face; and I looked into incredibly dark, smiling eyes.

Fifteen minutes later, Frank revealed that he was forty-six. He looked incredible, though – not in a way that made him look ten years younger, but in a smart, well groomed, man-of-his-age way. I noted that his jacket was of the most expensive leather. In fact everything about him smacked of sophistication and care – like a man out of a coffee advert. I was impressed.

The following evening, I was ready for my first date with him. He lived only a short distance away and even though he didn't have a car, he decided we should make a big event out of our first date and go into the West End. 'We'll take a cab,' he said, which was the way he usually travelled. It was fine by me.

By seven-thirty p.m. my dream date arrived, in a minicab, with a huge bunch of flowers. Thirty minutes later, we were laughing over 'Oliver Live'; we shared the same sense of humour – or so I thought.

By eleven-thirty we were on the way home; the cab which had brought us had returned for us. I was in two minds as to whether I should invite him in for coffee, dreading a wrong interpretation, but longing for the evening to go on. I plucked up the courage and asked, wouldn't he rather send the cab away and come in for coffee.

Once out of the cab I waited for him to go back and pay off the driver, but to my surprise, he said 'Let's make the coffee then,' and escorted me smartly into the foyer of my block of flats. 'What about the cab?' I asked; he simply smiled. Oh well, I thought, he must have an account with them.

Twenty minutes later, over hot steaming mugs of coffee, there was a knock on the door. When Frank whispered not to answer, it would be the cab driver, I still didn't understand. Ten minutes later, the irate driver's increasingly furious knocking must have woken the whole street, together with his threats to get the police so he could have his fare.

Frank laughed like a schoolboy, and urged me to turn off all the lights while we stayed hidden in the kitchen. Part of me wanted to offer to pay the fare myself; but the question remained, why didn't he pay him off?

After what seemed like an age, the banging and shouting stopped. Peeping out of the window down to the street, Frank announced that he'd gone. Then he began to mutter about the £30 fare being too steep and cab drivers who were unlicensed and uninsured being unable to call the police.

He assured me that he did it all the time. Taking the coffee cup out of my hands – I'd been clutching it helplessly for the last ten minutes – he asked me if I had anything stronger on offer.

I got up and told him he should leave. I think he sensed that I was not amused, this adolescent lout in a grown-up's leather jacket.

Lois F., 36, secretary

❦❦❦

I met Terry at a party and was instantly attracted to him. When he asked me out I was over the moon. Our first two dates were wonderful, so when he told me he was taking me somewhere special and close to his heart I had visions of a romantic setting, candles on the table, the whole bit.

I spent a *fortune* on a gorgeous new dress, plus countless hours on my hair and make-up. When I arrived at our meeting place I was feeling terrific. So it was a bit of a surprise to see Terry standing with a huge crowd of people, all of whom were wearing coats but no trousers. The biggest shock was when I saw that my date, whose big masculine body had first attracted me to him, was wearing stiletto heels.

Terry noticed me and shouted me over. 'You're a bit overdressed,' he said. He then pulled open his coat to reveal a basque, stockings and suspenders. 'Did I forget to mention to put your suspenders on? We're going to the Rocky Horror Show.'

Yes, you did forget, actually, Terry. I do hate unnecessary injury to my bank account. But the real trouble was – from then on, every time he called me I just kept seeing his hairy chest poking over the top of a black lace basque.

Call me old-fashioned, but as a passion-killing image that sure worked for me.

Jill K., 27, nursery school worker

I was eighteen years old, doing my A-levels at Tech and still living with my parents. One night, I was at a local pub and I got talking to this bloke called Mike. We seemed to get on really well – same interests, same tastes in music – so we exchanged telephone numbers.

The next day I got a call from him asking me if I'd like to go for a moonlight picnic. Very romantic. I accepted without hesitation (maybe that was my first mistake!). After a little more conversation he asked me if I wouldn't mind going halves on the petrol; he didn't get much money because he was a student. I thought it was a bit of a cheek, but I said OK because I hadn't been out for ages.

At seven o'clock there was a beep outside and I was all done up and raring to go. I got into the car to the tune of Guns N' Roses' 'Sweet Child O' Mine' and a compliment that went something like, 'You're looking thinner than you did last night.'

I wanted to get out of the car that instant, but everybody deserves a second chance.

We drove into the country, found a nice place to sit, and Mike got out the picnic basket. Credit where credit is due, he had gone to a lot of trouble.

Cheese and pickle sandwiches, two mini pork pies, four cheese and onion pasties and a bottle of Sainsbury's special offer white wine. No glasses so we had to drink out of the bottle.

After about an hour and a half he lifted his arm from my shoulder and said, 'I'm bursting for a slash, wine does that to me. I'll go behind that tree; you can come and hold it for me if you like.'

Needless to say I declined the offer. I decided that

perhaps when he came back we should go home.

We got in the car and headed back. Mike was blasting his Guns N' Roses tape and insisted on banging his head and singing along to it as he drove.

So he didn't see the pot-hole in the middle of the road.

There was a big bang as he drove into it, and we swerved into a ditch. The front tyre had blown and he didn't have a spare.

Great.

I spent the next four hours walking through muddy fields, riding in a pick-up truck and hanging around some badly lit garage while a snotty-nosed git of a mechanic found and fitted a new tyre to Mike's car.

I got home at three forty-five in the morning, extremely pissed off. To top it all I got a phone call from him the next day, asking me to pay £25 towards the tyre because the whole thing would never have happened if he hadn't taken me out!

I couldn't believe what I was hearing. I screamed some rather choice four-letter words at him (I believe that some words had more than four letters, come to think of it) and then slammed the phone down. But he kept ringing until I paid. That evening cost me £30 and was probably the worst night of my entire life. I don't think I'll be going on any more moonlight picnics again in a hurry.

Suzanne C., 20, student

I had known Martin for quite a while, and knew he wanted to ask me out even though I was a lot older than he was. When he finally built up the courage to get round to asking me I agreed, feeling flattered by a young man's attention.

Martin arranged for us to have a romantic evening together. A candle-lit dinner, best wine, the most elegant setting. I felt totally desirable. Martin was very loving and affectionate, his gorgeous deep dark eyes caressing me across the table and making my hormones go into overdrive, my imagination running riot as to what might be . . .

Martin suggested we finish off with a nightcap across the road in the village pub. Images of holding hands next to a log fire seemed very appealing.

I settled myself next to the open fire waiting for Martin to return with the drinks. Suddenly, there was a piercing shriek.

A lady standing at the bar had last spotted my date when out walking her dog on the local golf course. He was running around stark naked doing an impersonation of a tree.

I couldn't believe it.

I was dating the local flasher.

At least the police gave me a lift home.

Isabel M., 38, freelance writer

2
'Call this a good time?':
Disappointment 2

Several years ago, when I was working as a hotel
receptionist, I met a gorgeous man who was staying in
the hotel with a conference for a week. By the end of
the week we'd been out together once or twice and fallen
madly in lust. He arranged to come over the following
week on his day off, and take me for a day up on the
moors. He'd told me he liked walking, and I had visions
of a romantic stroll beside ravishing waterfalls and in
quiet meadows. I wore my tightest Levis and a fluffy,
feminine angora sweater, and tipped half a pint of Rive
Gauche over myself.

On the day, he collected me in his car, and we drove
out to the moors. He parked the car miles from
anywhere, and tenderly told me he'd bought me a
present. I ripped the paper off in sheer greed, only to
find a pair of hiking boots. 'I guessed your size,' he said
smugly. He'd guessed correctly – but in these enormous
boots, with my tight jeans, I closely resembled a Smurf.

When he'd said he liked walking, he hadn't meant
'walking' as in the 'stroll for two yards, call in at a pub
for cold cider' type of walking. He meant WALKING.
He strapped his own boots on and set off at a cracking
pace like Miss Jean Brodie, expecting me to keep up.
To someone like me, accustomed only to the type of

exercise involved in turning the pages of a book or lifting a forkful of pasta, it was a nightmare. In the angora jumper I was baking hot, and thank God I'd emptied all that perfume all over my body, because I was sweating like a sumo wrestler. My tight Levis felt like a vice.

Eventually, when he suggested lunch in a place 'just over that hill', I almost cried with relief; but 'that hill' turned out to be of Everest-like proportions. When I felt as if my heart was about to burst out of my ribcage, he finally said 'Here we are,' pointing ahead in triumph. I looked up, fully expecting to see a tiny little country inn with a thatched roof and ivy round the door. At the bottom of the hill, nestling in a gravel pit, was a lorry drivers' transport cafe. When I burst into hysterical laughter, certain he was joking, my date from hell said, 'They do the best bacon sandwiches for miles around.'

We held hands across a formica-topped table until a woman in an egg-stained apron with her teeth clamped round a cigarette like a gangster, slapped two doorstep sandwiches in front of us, together with thick mugs of orange tea. 'Enjoy,' she said. I have to confess, the bacon sandwiches were delicious, but after that marathon hike I think I could have eaten a plateful of dead mice.

The end of the ordeal was now in sight, and as my blood sugar level went back up, so did my tolerance level, and I began to think that the walk hadn't been so bad after all. My date leaned across the table and said the words I'd been longing to hear . . . 'I think I'm falling in love with you.' The only problem was, at that moment, a lorry driver in a grey vest rubbed his stomach and let out a rousing belch, which reduced me to fits of laughter. This was the point at which I discovered that my date didn't have a sense of humour – a danger sign which I ignored at that stage.

My nightmare date ended with a hair-raising drive home in thick fog which had descended from nowhere, with him showing off, going round corners in top gear and accelerating round hairpin bends like Nigel Mansell.

Did I see him again? I certainly did. I was too infatuated with him to worry about the fact that we had absolutely nothing in common, and that all he wanted to do was try to involve me in his own interests, while making no effort to involve himself in mine. Like a fool, I faked an interest in all things sporty, when in reality I preferred a night at the theatre. I still can't quite believe that I went through that ordeal to be rewarded solely by blisters the size of soup plates.

Julie E., 38, secretary

🌺🌺🌺

My date in hell was nearly a date in heaven – or would have been if Mike had got his way! I was trying to get over a broken heart, and my friend Jane had 'fixed me up' on a blind date with Mike, a grave-digger. As I was due to go off on holiday the next day I thought, Why not?

Mike roared up for our date clad in bold black leather on a big black bike. 'We'll go for a walk if you like,' he suggested. Being keen on fresh air and the outdoor life, I leapt on the back of the machine. We blasted off . . . in the direction of the cemetery where Mike worked.

We strolled through the cemetery, holding hands on the warm summer's evening. I thought that Mike seemed quite a gentleman, and conversation was flowing easily. 'I'll show you what I did today if you like, Sue,' he said. In a flash he had whipped away a sheet of corrugated steel from before my eyes, revealing a freshly dug grave.

I almost fell into the gaping pit while struggling for words to extol the virtues of his divine digging. Mike was obviously proud and, as graves go, it was pretty good and looked just like the ones I'd always seen on horror films.

The date moved on to a nearby village pub where we shared stories and lingered over drinks. One or two eerie stories about funereal life aside, he was nice and 'interesting', and when he suggested coffee at his parents' before dropping me home, I happily agreed. After all, I was off on my holiday the next morning and felt happy and relaxed.

Back on the bike, we zoomed back to his parents', where he told me that they too were away on holiday.

Alarm bells started to ring. 'Ay ay,' I thought, 'and you'd seemed so nice.'

Well, he duly made the coffees, and then announced that he was going upstairs to get a book which I might like to read on my coach journey the following day.

'Oh yeah,' I thought, 'and next you're gonna call me upstairs, same old tricks.'

Mike descended the stairs with two pamphlet-type

magazines. 'The Undertakers' Annual Conference magazine,' he said. 'You may be interested, Sue.' With trembling hands I leafed through the pages, aghast at the various types of 'triple cold storage' fridges and luxurious coffins available to the unsuspecting stiffs. The pages were filled with all sorts of accessories available, and Mike was positively quivering with excitement as each page turned.

I beat a hasty retreat from the grave-digger's house, but the next day on the coach, I ran out of interesting literature and thought of . . .

Sue R., 30, local council customer service officer

❦❦❦

The first time I met Kevin was at a friend's birthday celebration. I had been warned about him – I think the advice was 'ignore him'.

Very wise.

His first words were 'You've got really good dress sense.' Then he continued with a barrage of questions – how old was I, how much did I earn, what was my relationship with my brothers and sisters, how had my parents' divorce affected me? The worst thing was that I found myself answering him!

He then decided I should take him out to dinner since I earned more than he did (he was a poor medical student), and made me repeat his phone number over and over so I wouldn't forget it.

What a shame I have no head for figures.

Three months later, we met again. This time he told me how much we had in common and that if I went out with him I would have the best time ever. We were, er, made for each other. Apparently.

He phoned me several times during the next week. A Nobel Prize for whoever invented answerphones. I just happened to be 'out' every time the telephone rang.

Another three months passed until I saw him again, and once more he told me how I really ought to go out with him – I'd enjoy myself so much, etc. etc. At this point my friend interjected, 'Put him out of his misery and just go out with him once – it'll shut him up.' So muggins here, defences finally worn down, agrees and the date is arranged.

We met in a local pub for a couple of drinks before going on to dinner. To be fair I did enjoy myself at first, but it didn't last.

The conversation got round to the future – our future. He wanted to know what branch of medicine I wanted him to specialize in – it was important that we agree about this if our marriage (HEEELLPPP) was to be successful.

By the time we left the pub, it had been decided (by Kevin) where we would live, how many children we would have – and even the number of dogs we would own.

How I survived the meal which followed I don't know. Kevin showed me a scab the size of a fifty-pence piece on his arm which he got after an insect bite turned nasty. He also asked me every question you could ever think of asking someone – the best was 'How often do you masturbate?' This one stunned not only me into silence but also the couple at the next table.

And I was still feeling a bit queasy about the scab.

When the bill arrived, Kevin told me he'd run out of cash and had left his credit cards and cheque book at home – so 'Would you mind . . .?'

When we got off the bus on the way home he asked me if I wanted to go to his house, saying 'I'll drive you home in the morning.' I politely declined this kind, unselfish offer and off we trotted in the direction of my house. I was under the impression that he was just walking me home. How wrong I was.

When we reached my house, he asked if he could come in and use the bathroom.

Always a bit of a hard one to refuse.

In the meantime, I went to see if there were any messages for me, then went up to my room to take off my coat. Suddenly Kevin walked in, having just cleaned his teeth, took all his clothes off and got into my bed!

When I asked him what he thought he was doing he just said 'Going to bed'. I suggested that this was perhaps a little presumptuous, whereupon he said 'Oh, don't you want to have sex with me? You'll really enjoy it. Every girl I've slept with has.' It took two hours to convince him that I really didn't want to sleep with him, and he finally left.

Kevin phoned me the next day and I told him I didn't want to go out with anyone right now. (I know, I know. Why couldn't I just say 'In your *dreams*'.) He told me I needed cognitive therapy, whatever that may be, and that I'd be mad to pass him up.

Thought I'd take the risk.

Joanne P., 27, office manager

꿍-꿍-꿍

Unbeknown to me, my girlfriends had written to a radio 'lonely hearts' programme in order to 'fix me up'. The first I knew about it was when I received a letter from Bill.

We corresponded for a few weeks and then decided to meet. The arrangements were made and I arrived in the said pub car park and waited.

Shortly after, a van pulled in. I did not pay much attention, as Bill said he would be in a 'sporty little number'. Imagine my surprise when it turned out to be him. We said our hellos, and when I questioned his description of his transport, he said it was the speed that was classed as sporty, not the vehicle.

Frankly, he was rather given to questionable descriptions. He'd claimed to be 6ft 2in tall, broad with blond hair, green eyes and a 'devilishly handsome face'. In fact, he was only slightly bigger than my 5ft 7in, thinner than me, with mousy hair and pale blue eyes. As for 'devilishly handsome', well – not *exactly* . . .

Not to worry, I thought, nothing ventured, nothing gained.

We were going on to a concert later (a surprise), but would just have one drink in the pub beforehand. I asked for a glass of white wine and felt slightly awkward when he ordered a glass of tap water for himself. Still, I said to myself, he was driving.

The pub was quite crowded, and I nearly choked on my own teeth when he said loudly, 'Well, you are smashing, what do you think of me?' as he twirled around with arms outstretched. The people nearest to us all stopped what they were doing and just stared. Then a few began to giggle. But it was the pitying looks that were the worst.

I finished my drink and he announced, again in a loud voice, 'You are not having another, I don't want you getting out of control in the van.'

I made up the excuse of needing something from my car in order to get away. On the way out, I actually had it all planned to drive home and end it all. (The relationship, not my life. Though I wasn't too sure at the time.) The next thing I heard was 'Cooee', and there he was, coming after me. He said it was about time we started off for the concert.

I wondered who would be playing, as it was still a surprise. But he knew what music I liked and so I felt confident enough.

As he opened the van, I heard some noises that weren't too familiar at first. But the smell definitely was. When I peered in, I saw I would be sharing the ride with half a dozen pigs.

We drove to the venue in relative silence, with the windows down. He actually had the cheek to say, 'I'm glad you are a non-smoker, I can't stand the smell.'

I asked why we were bringing the pigs. Fond of music, were they? He said their sty was being renovated and this was their new home. Anyway, he knew I was an animal lover.

Just as we were pulling into the car park, he started to get all excited, saying how much he loved this group. My first clue. I tried to think who he liked, and remembered they were who I liked: Duran Duran, The

Human League, Spandau Ballet . . .

Going in, I tried to see who was on, but the posters around were of various artists, and he steered me clear of the T-shirt and poster-sellers. So by the time we sat down I still had no idea who it was.

Suddenly, the group were on stage and I nearly died, as I recognized . . .

It's probably libellous to say which is the tackiest and most pathetic band in the entire universe. But – it was them.

Thought I'd go and sit with the pigs.

Kath R., 31, nurse / midwife

❧❧❧

I had seen Greg at the garage – he'd worked there for about four months. Every morning on my way to work he would smile and say hello. One morning he asked me if I would like to go out for a meal with him. He seemed ever so nice and attractive, and I said yes.

As the date got closer, I started getting really excited. It took quite a while to decide what to wear . . . Something that showed off my good points . . . That little black thing would be just right.

He'd said he'd pick me up at eight. The time came and he pulled up in a van. The inside was a charming mixture of mud, dog hairs, empty sweet wrappers and crushed beer cans. I climbed in carefully. Then he said, 'Do you mind if I stop on the way? It won't take long, but my friend's car has broken down.'

When we arrived at his friend's house he got out, and slipped his blue overalls on top of his clothes. I couldn't believe it. Of course, I stayed in the car. He kept saying, 'Just ten more minutes.' After an hour I was getting really fed up. I was thinking about leaving when he said, 'We are just putting everything back now. It won't take long.' But of course his hands and face were covered in oil, and it took him fifteen minutes to clean up.

When eventually he came out of the house, he was not alone. 'I hope you don't mind, but I have invited my friend along,' he said. 'He hasn't got anyone to go out with tonight.'

We arrived at a pub that looked as though it had been chewed up and spat out. I looked, let's say, over-dressed.

My date and his friend spent the whole evening talking about cars. I might as well not have been there, he wouldn't have noticed.

When he dropped me off, he said, 'Thanks for a lovely time. Can we do it again?'

Maggie H., 23, secretary

❦❦❦

My first date with Stuart was great; we went to a quiet country pub, chatted all evening and had a pleasant goodnight kiss on my doorstep. I happily agreed to go out with him the following Saturday for the day. 'I'm going to surprise you,' he grinned. And didn't he just.

We drove to the country, up into the hills, which would have been nice except that it was pouring with rain and he couldn't read the road signs so we went completely the wrong way. He got crosser and crosser. That was the start.

He eventually calmed down a bit when we reached our destination, a village in the middle of nowhere. Whereupon he turned to me triumphantly, saying 'I bet you don't know where we are.' I shook my head. It looked pretty boring to me, and I was dying for the loo in any case.

But I dutifully followed him towards a church, presuming there was a ten-screen cinema or ten-pin bowling alley behind it. But no, we went into the church, and he then informed me exactly where we were.

'This is the town where the bubonic plague started,' he announced. I stared at him. 'In this church,' he continued, 'they actually have a bit of cloth from the house where it started. Isn't that fascinating?' I stared at him harder. Sounded disgusting to me.

But still I played along, following him round, exclaiming excitedly at said cloth, gazing at a chair that someone had once sat on, a cup that someone had once sipped from, and wished I was elsewhere.

After ONE HOUR in that church, he dragged me to the cottage where it all began, and we stood in the rain reading endless plaques on the wall.

Finally, we returned to the car. It was nearly two o'clock and I was bored, dying for the loo still and absolutely starving. So we stopped at a pub. The menu wasn't very exciting – in fact the only thing on it that

I liked was beefburger with garnish and chips. In my present state, it sounded marvellous. Stuart turned to me. 'What do you fancy?' I beamed at him and said in a breathy voice, 'I'd just love beefburger with garnish and chips.' Don't ask me why, but he thought I was being sarcastic. 'No, I don't fancy anything either. Drink up and we'll go.'

Next stop was B & Q because he wanted a bag of cement. That took about half an hour. Then we went to a pub for a Coke and a bag of crisps. That was lunch.

We then drove home, and I was in such a foul mood I didn't say a word to him, until we passed a Beefeater restaurant. 'Stop here!' I screamed. He did, bless him, and turned to me. 'Can we please eat?' I gasped. 'I'll die if I don't eat.' He smiled engagingly. 'Then we shall eat.'

So we ordered our food. I chose the most expensive item on the menu, and asked for wine. 'Just one glass,' Stuart told the waiter. I glared at him.

Now, this is the horrific part of the day. My single glass of wine appeared. I had one sip and placed it on the table. We were sitting in silence, he couldn't seem to think of one thing to say, and instead he started picking his ear. I don't mean just a quick scratch, I mean his finger was plunged in to the hilt. As I sat watching him in total disbelief, the contents of his ear started to fall on the table, perilously close to my single glass of wine. Well, I snatched it pretty fast, then decided not to risk a sip in case I had blinked and missed a small chunk actually dropping in. Feeling faint, I excused myself and dashed to the loo.

I chain-smoked two cigarettes, walked back out, and

stood smiling sweetly at him. 'Stuart,' I said, 'I really think you should take me home.'

Alison J., 27, retail manager

❧❧❧

I was delighted when Chris asked if he could come to the city to see me. I'd met him in a pub in a small village miles away, and it was flattering that he should want to travel such a long distance just to visit me.

I was slightly perturbed, however, when I met him at the railway station – he was a foot shorter than me. In the pub we had both been seated, and in a haze of alcohol my judgement had been blurred. All the same, I convinced myself, looks can be deceiving, and he's come all this way after all.

After we had exchanged a few pleasantries, Chris suggested a visit to a friend of his. I agreed readily. He must be keen on me if he's introducing me to his friends already, I thought.

As I entered the friend's flat, I found myself surrounded by a narcotic haze. The room was blue with smoke because ten youths were seated, passing round a joint. Eagerly, Chris produced money and exchanged it with the 'friend' for the largest chunk of hash I had ever seen. I was beginning to feel dismayed.

Three hours later, after repeatedly being offered hash and being forced to watch a Western on TV, I was positively angry. Chris was absorbed in his drugs – no wonder he'd been prepared to make such a long journey

– and had completely forgotten my existence. After several pointed hints, I made my escape – unfortunately with Chris still in tow.

He could hardly speak and seemed quite docile, so foolishly I invited him back to my flat for a cup of coffee.

On entering, he miraculously regained the power of speech. 'Is it OK if I stay the night?' he demanded.

I began to frame a polite negative.

'But I've missed the last bus home,' he pleaded plaintively. Reluctantly I said yes, upon which he pulled a pair of purple Y-fronts out of his pocket and uttered the immortal words, 'I came prepared!'

I didn't know what to say.

All evening I was entertained with comments along the lines of: 'Imagine if a wasp flew down your pants and stung your nuts!'

He also treated me to his belch rendition of 'London's Burning'.

The flat had no sitting-room and the hall was like the Arctic. I was too humane to make him sleep out there, so I made a great display of arranging a sleeping bag on my bedroom floor – at as far a distance as possible from my bed.

He refused to observe my tactful hints. I spent a memorable night warding off his enthusiastic advances and vowing never, ever to speak to men in pubs again.

Fiona A., 20, student

Things like this didn't usually happen to someone like me. The anticipation began as soon as I opened my eyes. What should I wear? It's a bit difficult to find an outfit for a first rendezvous with a fanciable man, that's also something you can wear for a whole morning at a busy dental clinic, drilling and filling teeth – all without looking like you're ready to go down the disco! I eventually made my choice, along with a ridiculously high-heeled pair of shoes which were saved purely for those 'special occasions'.

Off I tottered in the direction of the dental school, wondering how I would ever last the three-and-a-half hours until lunch time. My mind was certainly not on my amalgam fillings that morning.

Lunchtime arrived. I zipped out of the hospital, leaving my classmates going to the hospital canteen. Tuna and mayonnaise rolls with a cup of stewed coffee for them, I presumed, as I pictured my forthcoming culinary delights: smoked salmon, strawberries and cream, accompanied perhaps by a chilled glass of champagne. In a totally sumptuous setting, of course.

He was waiting for me in his car. Something made me a little uneasy as I got in. Why did I get an uncomfortable feeling? Was he leering at me? I must be imagining it . . . it must be nerves . . . just relax . . . you're over-reacting!

'I thought we'd head out of town a few miles to a little pub I know,' he began.

'Great.' ('Little pub'? Oh well, could still be a gem of exquisite cuisine, in all the restaurant guides . . .)

'I'll just have to stop off at the petrol station first –

the tank's really low. I should have filled up this morning.'

'No problem.'

He started the engine and we drove off, leaving the hospital behind.

'I must be really getting to the bottom of the tank,' he said. 'It's a good job the garage is down here.'

Famous last words as the car ground to a halt.

'We'll have to walk to the garage. I'll see if I can borrow a petrol can and get it filled up. It's only just down the road.'

Never mind, I thought, it won't be long and then we'll be back on our way. We got out of the car and started walking.

We walked . . .

and walked . . .

and walked . . .

and my feet in my ludicrous high heels began to hurt . . .

and then they began to hurt a bit more.

What on earth had made me put these shoes on?

We passed rows of houses . . .

shops . . .

more houses . . .

We finally got to the garage.

Then we turned around and repeated the trek of the century.

By the time we finally got back to the car, I was windswept and my feet were killing me. To add insult to injury, we only had time to go somewhere quite local.

We started off again, delivered the petrol can back to the garage, got stuck in some traffic and, by the time we reached our destination (a pub with all the charm of a used Hoover bag), all we had time for was a quick half of lager.

I began to realize what I'd let myself in for as he leered and loomed in on me in the car parked outside the pub – the stewed cup of coffee and stale sandwich in the staff canteen were suddenly becoming a seriously attractive option.

If this was excitement, thrills and romance, you could keep it! I couldn't believe I'd let myself be taken in and I couldn't wait for this ordeal to be over.

I'd had more fun pulling out teeth.

Melissa U., 29, dentist

🐝🐝🐝

I was getting ready for my second date with Tim when the phone rang – it was him. He asked if instead of having a meal out as planned, we could rearrange it for his home because he felt like cooking that evening. I felt wary, and wondered whether it was just an invitation to bed. However, on our previous date Tim had told me he had been a chef many years ago, and described some of his mouthwatering recipes. I was tired and hungry after an awful day at work and so I relented and agreed.

When I arrived at his home, Tim greeted me at the door with a large striped apron covering his jeans. I was a little perturbed to see the apron was spotless. Surely if he was preparing this gourmet meal there should be food stains on it. Still, I thought, perhaps that's the way professional chefs look.

The table was beautifully set, and after a short while Tim rushed in dramatically with the meal. I smiled with anticipation . . . only to see two small foil packages on the very large elegant plates. A frozen dinner, reheated.

Still, food isn't everything.

Tim had told me a lot about what he had done in the past, but I didn't know exactly how he did earn a living now. In fact, he had been a little evasive about it. To my horror, he revealed that he sold incontinence aids for women.

He then went on to explain all the gory details of why and how women became incontinent.

By now I didn't feel at all hungry, and any romantic feelings had quite disappeared.

After dinner, we went to sit on a couple of armchairs by the fireplace. Suddenly, Tim leaned forward and stared into my eyes. 'I want to have a child,' he said. I was so amazed that I nearly fell off the chair, and then he did a flying leap across the rug and landed on me, saying 'I want to marry you and have a baby.'

As I didn't answer, because I was finding it difficult to breathe, he said that if I had any problems after having the child he could always provide an endless supply of incontinence aids.

I wrestled him off and charged out of his flat, with Tim calling out 'What about your dessert, it's strawberries.'

When I turned round, I saw him in hot pursuit, his stripy apron waving in the wind, carrying the strawberries. Suddenly I saw a bus appear along the High Street and leapt on it. Tim just caught up in time, shouting 'You've forgotten these.' And so, to the amazement of the other passengers, I grabbed the bowl of strawberries as the bus was driving off and waved him goodbye, for ever.

Vicki F., 31, secretary

❦❦❦

My romance with Roger started in a sweetly innocent, romantic kind of way. I used to answer our firm's switchboard occasionally; Roger worked at another of our branches, and would call our office frequently.

As time went on, we became more chatty with each other. We also managed to find out through mutual colleagues that we were both single. So one Saturday I had a lovely surprise when a single red rose was delivered to my home. The rose was quickly followed by a phone call from Roger, suggesting an evening out together. A date was arranged.

I was impressed. Not only by the rose, but also by the fact that a man wanted to take me out to dinner. It made such a change from the usual half-of-lager-and-a-packet-of-crisps treatment I had been used to.

So I arrived at our designated meeting place, nervous but quietly excited. It was a totally 'blind' date, as neither of us had actually met before. But I knew that I liked what I had so far heard about him from our numerous and lengthy telephone conversations.

He arrived on time, in a nice car and dressed fairly smartly. I breathed a sigh of relief on seeing that he looked OK, too.

As the arrangement was for dinner, I was secretly hoping for a nice, quiet, romantic restaurant. Soft music, subtle lighting and wonderful food.

The reality . . .

I found myself in a 'greasy spoon' style cafe, complete with hideously patterned plastic tablecloths, tomato sauce bottles and tatty menus in worn plastic jackets.

Being totally amazed at Roger's choice of eaterie, and too meek to complain, I let him order for me. I was too stunned for words when he confidently ordered two of the 'Three Course Specials at a discount price'.

The meal got the award for the dullest combination ever – soup (dishwater with worm-like noodles floating in it), roast beef (dead from natural causes) and apple pie (at a guess).

The conversation between us was even more boring: the weather, his car, his hamster, the weather, his boss, the weather. He'd obviously shot his conversational bolt in our phone talks.

I knew that our date was turning into a first-rate disaster, and my opinion of Roger was heading downhill fast.

After the meal, not wanting to prolong the agony any further, I was determined to head home as soon as possible to forget about the whole nightmarish evening. So I managed to feign a good headache ('It's the spots in front of the eyes I find so awful') and we set off back to his car.

While we were walking the short way to the car park, Roger decided that I needed entertaining with his brilliant impressions. Now, personally, I am not against a good impression of someone worth impersonating. But Roger's repertoire was fairly limited.

I found myself talking to Kermit the Frog. As well as I could, that is, given my cringing embarrassment as passers-by stared at Roger in amazement – obviously thinking to themselves, 'Poor woman, fancy being stuck with that idiot.'

The drive home was long but, thankfully, absolutely silent.

Cindy E., 31, personal assistant

🐸🐸🐸

About seven years ago I placed an ad in our local paper to meet a man for a meaningful relationship. I had been divorced for about five years, and had grown very disillusioned with the sort of men you can meet in pubs and discos.

I had loads of replies – amongst them a pleasant letter from a man who sounded very outgoing. The photo enclosed was also most promising, so I rang him and we had a long chatty conversation. We arranged that he would collect me on the Friday evening to go out for a drink. Just before he rang off he said, 'Oh by the way, I hope you won't be put off but I work for an undertaker.'

Trying to keep an open mind and not wanting to

appear shallow, I replied, 'Of course not – someone's got to do it.'

Friday came, a glorious, sunny, hot day. I dressed carefully, not wanting to over- or under-dress. At about seven-thirty p.m. an enormous, black, shiny hearse drew up outside my flat.

Panic and embarrassment set in. All my neighbours were extremely nosy and always had a good look if I was seen going out with a man.

I opened the front door and introduced myself – slightly disappointed because the driver did not live up to the promise of the photo. 'Hi, I'm Ben,' he said. 'I've bought you some strawberries.'

Great, I thought. Then suddenly I smelt an unusual, sickly aroma coming from his direction. Could it be embalming fluid? My appetite disappeared.

'I hope you don't mind,' he said, 'if we drop off at work so I can pick up my car? Then we'll go have a good time.' What could I say without appearing rude – I've never liked hurting people's feelings.

I braced myself as we left the flat and got in the hearse. I felt ridiculous. We drove the four miles to his workplace – the longest drive of my life as everyone we passed stared in at us.

Finally, we arrived at the funeral parlour. We put the hearse in the garage and walked round to the entrance. 'I have to collect a few things first. Let me give you a tour,' he said.

Embarrassment started to turn to panic. 'Lovely,' I gasped. We entered the first room. 'This is where I dress the clients,' he said, pointing to the wooden benches. By this time I could only smile weakly. The next room was the chapel of rest. With its two coffins. Occupied.

Call this a good time?

Dazed, I found myself in his car on our way to the pub. Ben's conversation revolved around undertaking: shroud colours, coffin styles, the latest make-up techniques for the dead.

At long last the evening was over.

Eternity had been the only word for it.

Lindsey R., 41, housewife

🐾🐾🐾

A friend of mine had been raving for weeks about an acquaintance of her boyfriend, who, by all accounts, was exceptionally good-looking. I met him briefly in the pub one night, agreed immediately with all the reports regarding his stunning looks, and accepted with alacrity when he asked me to spend the day with him the following Saturday.

After carefully washing and ironing one of my best outfits I went to bed early on Friday night, full of high hopes. I was determined to look my best in the morning and make a good impression.

The first hint of what was to follow came when Keith rang my doorbell at seven-thirty on the Saturday morning, catching me in my old and grey Snoopy nightie, hair all over the place, and no make-up on.

Nevertheless, I graciously invited him in to wait while I showered and dressed at breakneck speed, abandoning my long soak in the bath and hour-long session in front of the mirror making myself look beautiful.

Things began to look up as we drove out into the country and parked by the riverbank. Keith began to unload boxes and hampers from the boot of the car, as I began to imagine romantic champagne picnics and long kisses by the river. I could only stare in horror as he energetically began to unpack fishing rods, tackle, and a compartmentalized box full of writhing maggots.

Happily settled on his folding stool, he spent the next few hours spearing maggots with a fish hook and casting his line. Every time I tried to get a conversation going I was met with a stern glare and a rebuke that talking would scare away the fish. The entire Saturday morning was spent in absolute silence with Keith gazing peacefully out across the river, while I sat sulking on a tree stump, getting angrier and angrier, gazing in the other direction.

After four exceptionally boring hours, during which I managed to count every blade of grass in sight, Keith announced that it was lunchtime. Having missed breakfast, thanks to his premature arrival that morning, I was by now starving and dreaming of a sumptuous picnic.

Wrong again. Keith reached into his haversack and pulled out a jam sandwich and a banana, which he handed to me with a flourish.

By now I was seething and demanded that he take me home. Looking slightly hurt, he agreed, but told me that he'd promised to call in on his mother on the way home. I was too defeated and weary to argue and after a very awkward journey, we duly pulled up at his mother's house.

As soon as I met her things, unbelievably, went from bad to worse. Whereas Keith could do no wrong in her eyes, she proceeded to criticize everything about me, from my clothes to my job, and ended up with the classic 'You're not as pretty as Keith's last girlfriend.'

That was absolutely the last straw. Finally losing my temper I snapped, 'I'm not his girlfriend and neither am I ever likely to be!' I then stormed off to wait in the car until Keith came out and proceeded to chastise me for being rude to his mother.

Pulling up outside my house I almost cried with relief. The worst date of my life was over! I'd never be taken in by good looks again. I leapt out of the car and sprinted up the path to the safety of my home. Keith had the last word, however. Pulling away from the kerb he leaned out of the window and said 'Thanks for coming out with me, but if you don't mind, I don't think we'll do this again – you're not really my type!'

Mandy W., 26, bar person

3
'I took one look':
Disappointment 3

On Looks Alone

OK, OK, maybe joining Dateline isn't everyone's idea
of a cool way to meet blokes. But I had just left my self-
centred, temperamental, unaffectionate Irishman (for
the third time) and I wanted a replacement. I remember
filling in the questionnaire thinking, 'I'll show you, you
bastard!'

So of course I was delighted when, a couple of weeks
later, Simon called me. He had a good sense of humour,
seemed quite well educated, had a motorbike, did an
interesting job, described himself as tall and slim, and
lived about fifteen miles away. So far so good! After
chatting on the phone for the best part of an hour and
getting on really well, we decided the best thing to do
would be to meet. Being an unselfish soul, I volunteered
to hop on the train to his home town. We made the
arrangements and when I put the receiver down I was
glowing. I hadn't felt this excited for years!

Come the Big Day, nerves shredded, but full of eager
anticipation (having just had a Badedas bath), I arrived
at his station. The rendezvous point was the bookstall,
and I approached it with hope in my heart. A thousand
thoughts were spinning round my head: 'Will he like

me?' 'Will I dare kiss him?' 'What shall we call our first child?'

There were one or two people hanging around: an old lady with a shopping trolley, a couple of young lads, a nerdy-looking bloke in an anorak. I glanced around as casually as I could, hoping that Simon wouldn't be too long. At this point, I noticed that Anorak Man was looking at me in a peculiar way. I tried to avoid eye contact. Then I realized he was getting closer. He was beaming. He was carrying a bunch of flowers. He introduced himself. He was Simon.

Devastated is too inadequate a word to sum up my feelings. Simon was, to look at, everything I personally find unattractive in a man. He was painfully skinny, balding, and had a long, tatty beard – clearly the nest of several generations of local birdlife.

What did I do? I couldn't run away; I was too weak with sheer disappointment. So I smiled (wanly, I suspect) and introduced myself, thanking him for the flowers (polite despite wanting to die on the spot). He suggested that we go for a coffee. Now was the moment I needed that flash of inspiration, that brilliant, totally plausible excuse. 'I'm sorry, but I don't drink fluids.' Inspiration never came. We went for a coffee. As we walked along together, I kept trying to transmit to passers-by, via psychic rays, the message 'He's not *with* me, he just happens to be walking next to me.'

I'm not entirely sure how I coped for the rest of the afternoon. We sat in the square and talked; I tried to disguise myself. I told him about my job, my family, my friends, the village where I lived. He told me about his motorbike. After two or three months (or so it seemed) I managed to come up with a perfectly believable reason why I had to go. I needed to get home because my elderly, disabled next-door neighbour would be requiring me to help her use the commode.

I told Simon I'd enjoyed our date and said I'd get in touch soon. He kindly walked me to the train, and as it pulled away, an enormous wave of euphoria engulfed me as I realized that I would never, *ever* have to see him again.

Within ten minutes of getting home I had written him a letter saying that he was a lovely chap, but not really my type; and that was that. Call me cruel, call me heartless – I probably deserve it (because he *was* quite nice, personality-wise). But it sure was a date from hell.

And did I kiss him? Well, would *you* kiss a man wearing an orange anorak?!

Melanie L., 31, magazine designer

ೲೲ

I'd answered the phone to a man who wanted to speak to my flatmate, a colleague of hers from work. I said I was sorry, but she was out. He had a deep, syrupy, luscious, sexy voice. We started talking. We talked for an hour. We had so much in common: loved walking, films with subtitles, small children. 'I'd really like to meet you,' he said. 'Right now.'

'Oh,' I trilled, quite beside myself with excitement by this time, 'please do come round.'

Half an hour later, the bell went. I rushed for the door, flung it open, looked up – no one there. I looked down. On the doorstep stood a man about 5ft 3in tall (I'm 5ft 10in). Thin body, wispy beard and eyes bulging with an eager light. For me, the sex appeal of a water rat. I was so crushed with disappointment that I nearly lost another 7in myself.

Susie C., 36, account executive

❧❧❧

Me, I was naive, young and a student. And, what's more, all too consciously aware that for a full year I'd been one of a small minority who hadn't had a 'steady', or, to be honest, *any* kind of a boyfriend.

Anyway, out of the blue another of the 'unfortunate few' announced that her brother (a student of medicine – definitely in the good catch category) was inviting us to a student ball.

Excitement was mounting, as were the green hues emanating from the 'experienced' side of the common room as they got wind of our conversation. Unanswerable questions floated: 'What will we wear?' – 'Could this break our man-free run?' – 'Have I time to diet?' – 'How much can I go into debt over a dress?' – 'Will there be lots of eligible student doctors there?' All these and a trillion more were endlessly discussed.

Scene set – dance day loomed – excitement now at fever pitch. The group agreed to meet outside the appointed venue. Giggling was non-stop – moans of 'I

need the loo for the third time' – borrowed shoes
pinched – and thrilled shivers abounded. Everyone was
'glammed up' enough to look a little older. All arrived?
Yes. So in we trooped to the hall. Huge dance floor.
Rainbow colours. Stomachs butterflied. Nervous smiles
flickered and large eyes surveyed the whole scene –
and all those faces we didn't know.

One gorgeous brother appeared from the dance floor
to greet us, and his sister dragged us all after him. We
were hastily introduced to a group of males. There was
apparently one each, and automatically everyone
seemed to pair off as the two groups merged.

Until the last guy was left, sitting alone. He rather
awkwardly (or was it reluctantly?) signalled for me to
join him. Looking back he did seem a little resigned to
his fate, with a facial expression that said it all. Only I
refused to let it penetrate.

We eventually got quite chatty, and he seemed nice.
Drinks were ordered, and some of our group got up to
dance.

After an hour or so when the conversation was
wearing thin, my eyes drifted to the dancing.

Why didn't he ask me? Would he take a hint, I
wondered?

No.

To hell with trying to be subtle. I turned the chat to
discos. 'Where do you go?' 'Are you a good dancer?'

After much persistence he got the message. 'Do you
really want to dance?' he asked, sounding deeply
unenthusiastic.

'Yes please!'

I took his hand and pulled him up.

Oh no. I was getting ready to dance with his navel.
He was 6ft 4in – and I'm only 5ft 1in.

Floor please open up.

Everyone around us was laughing. His embarrassment added to my own, and it was the longest single track of music ever danced.

It was doomed from the start.

We did manage a few dates, and stolen kisses with the help of staircases. But laughing eyes followed us round, and I couldn't get rid of a self-conscious urge to stand on tiptoe the whole time.

I was probably his worst nightmare – the titch from hell – as he was mine. Heights of passion? Not for me. Depths of despair this time around, I fear.

Gail R., 34, mother / housewife

🐝🐝🐝

Looks – And The Rest

I was manager of a very small company at the time. Happily unattached, I was. My colleagues didn't think so. Kindly (oh, sure), they scoured the local lonely hearts column while I was at lunch.

One ad proved irresistible:

Handsome, solvent man is searching for the Woman In My Life. Please write with photo.

Unbelievably, they did. They even had the brass nerve to volunteer me to take the post that night, so I unwittingly mailed my own application to be The

Woman In His Life, for heaven's sake. Leaving the office, I heard a tide of skirt-caught-in-knickers type tittering.

I checked. It wasn't. Why, oh why wasn't I more suspicious?

Three days later, Barbara called excitedly across the office.

'Ellie, call for you on line three.'

'Who is it?'

'Won't give his name. Sounds dead sexy!'

The sexy-sounding ones usually have terminal halitosis and monster blackheads.

I sighed.

'Good morning, sir. Can I help you?'

'If you're as attractive as your photograph, you certainly can.'

I squashed the urge to throw up.

'Thank you, I'll certainly try. What can I do for you?'

'I loved your letter. Le Jardin is my favourite restaurant, too.'

Bemused, I repeated in the manner of a strangled African Grey: 'You loved my letter. Le Jardin is your favourite restaurant, too . . .?'

Behind me, frantic whispers.

'You'll have to tell her.'

'She'll go mad.'

'You tell her. You wrote the letter.'

I politely asked him to hold the line and fixed them with A Look.

They told me.

'Are you mad?' I yelled. 'This man's a client.'

'We didn't know. It was a box number.'

61

Oh great. I lined them up against the wall and shot them. No, not really, just felt like it.

I'm ashamed to confess, however, that the lure of a free meal proved overpowering. I agreed to meet him for lunch. My esteemed colleagues hung out of the windows, jostling for a glimpse of this catch.

I took one look, then ran to the car and growled 'Drive!' Not because he was so handsome. Oh, no. And he'd omitted to add 'weighs about twenty-eight stone, looks like a cross between a sumo wrestler and a bloodhound and has his suits made by a hot-air balloon company'. Fingers like peeled jumbo sausages.

I looked over my shoulder at a row of open mouths. I trusted they would spend their lunch break applying for new jobs.

I prayed nobody in Le Jardin would know me. I hid in a booth. I visited the ladies' eight times. I invented rampant toothache to allow me to cover my face with a scarf. I vowed to give up Crunchie bars if someone would get me out of there.

I can hear you saying, 'You *bitch*. Perhaps he had a wonderful personality.' Didn't see it, I'm afraid.

This man ate his starter in under one minute. He didn't stop talking once, his face uncomfortably close to mine. I windscreen-wiped specks of paté and crumbs of toast from my glasses. He had one topic of conversation: himself.

He ended the lunch by saying he wanted to see me again. Soon.

I lied.

'There's been a mistake. I'm married.'

He didn't care.

'My husband's a police inspector,' I said confidently.

He'd come round when my husband was on shift.

'I've got three children,' I shrieked.

He loved kids.

'My mother lives with us,' cried I, desperate.

He'd love to meet her.

I left through the kitchens. Fast.

He turned up in my local pub that night in a shiny suit, for God's sake. It was a parachute in a former life. For three months he pestered me. Two good friends of mine finally warned him off. So please, don't try this at home!

Ellie M., 37, self-employed businesswoman

❧❧❧

My two middle-aged aunts returned from a holiday in Europe bursting with excitement – they'd found me a man! 'Most people get a stick of rock,' I remarked, but they weren't to be deterred.

'We know we shouldn't have,' they apologized, 'but he was so charming, such good company. He's divorced and on his own, so when we told him our niece was too, he was so eager to meet you that we gave him your telephone number.'

'What's this dreamboat's name?' I asked. 'Harold,' they chorused with stars in their eyes.

Well, Harold rang the next evening. I couldn't tell much from his voice over the telephone but agreed to go for a drink with him. One night wouldn't hurt me, and I was curious to see this handsome brute my aunts had come back drooling over.

The big day arrived. He was due to pick me up at eight o'clock, so my mother arrived to baby-sit at a quarter to. She distributed sweets to the kids then settled herself into an armchair.

'Hadn't you better be getting ready?' she started. 'I am ready, Mother,' I answered. 'Oh, you're not getting dressed up then,' she went on, eyeing me up and down. 'Well, do your hair before he comes.' 'It's done, Mother,' I said between clenched teeth. 'Oh . . . what colour do you call those tights?' she asked, frowning.

My date arrived on the dot bearing a box of Dutch chocolates with an artificial rose he'd attached to them. If I'd seen him coming up the path I don't think I would have opened the door. I was a very young thirty-year-old and he was an old fifty-year-old, so we had an age gap of about thirty years between us! Mother started straightening her clothes, patting her perm and looking dewy-eyed at the plastic rose on the coffee table, so I bundled him out of the house.

I spent the next two hours hearing all about his holidays, his vasectomy, his ex-wife and his lodgings, desperately trying to hide behind a beer mat in case anyone should walk in to the pub and recognize me.

'Next time you go away,' I later informed my aunts, 'please just bring me a stick of rock.'

Becky V., 45, child care officer

🌺🌺🌺

When I started my new job at a posh hotel, I immediately noticed the nice-looking trainee assistant manager. I began to try to catch his attention at every opportunity. My friendly smiles soon paid off and he asked me if I'd like to go out with him one night.

We arranged to meet outside the cinema at eight p.m., and from the moment I arrived, I completely went off him! His first words were, 'I've been here since seven-fifteen. I like to be punctual.'

He then produced a half-eaten bag of Thorntons' Turkish Delights from his pocket, saying 'These are for you. Oh, but I have eaten one or two of them.'

The next blow came when I looked down at his feet. He was wearing the most horrendous pair of slip-on shoes that I've ever seen in my life – with white socks. Along with the half-ton of Brylcreem that he'd slapped on his head and the 'dodgy' yellow anorak he was wearing, he was just a complete fashion disaster.

He'd always looked so normal when in his uniform. And was too far across a crowded foyer to talk to.

Christine H., 25, hotel receptionist

❦❦❦

It started with a reply to an advertisement I had placed in the personal column of a local paper. I live in a small village, and do not have much opportunity to meet single eligible males. Forty-five, he said he was, worked for a brewery and was fit, solvent and attractive. Sounds OK, I thought.

We arranged to meet for dinner at my best local hotel. He would be driving a maroon-coloured car and he gave me the registration number.

I took a great deal of trouble with my appearance. I parked at the entrance to the car park and spent fifteen minutes scrutinizing all the arrivals. A maroon Mercedes pulled into the car park – I got quite excited, but then I realized the occupant had a wife or girlfriend with him. Shortly after this another maroon car approached. The driver seemed to be an elderly gentleman, the car something ancient and unrecognizable. He spotted me and waved.

When he got out of his car my heart sank into my boots. He had either deducted twenty years off his age, or, if he was really forty-five, then time had been very cruel to him.

He was wearing a zip-up cardigan over a frayed-at-the-collar shirt. His trousers fastened under his enormous (beer) belly and his shoes had at one time been sand-coloured suede. They were now well-splattered, with what I did not like to imagine. He was very cheerful, though.

I knew this hotel well, and immediately decided there was no way I was going to be seen in the restaurant with this man. But he gave my hand an energetic shake and then propelled me up the steps into the hotel. There were no dark corners in this beautifully lit bar. In desperation I selected the corner farthest from the bar and we sat down to drink our respective drinks.

He informed me that he had nowhere to stay for the night. I decided to ignore this remark. Over the next hour I learned all there is to know about brewing beer, twice over. I explained away my yawning by saying I had been up since five that morning.

The 'nowhere to stay' problem cropped up again. I said that this hotel should have rooms, but he had asked at the bar how much they were and they were much too expensive. I suggested we go and find him a cheaper room. He looked disappointed, and even more so when I insisted on going in my own car (on inspection, his car seemed to be held together with 'humorous' stickers, string and nicotine, not to mention the beer barrels in the rear) and that he should follow me.

Eventually we found him a room in a cheap hotel, and I booked a table at an Indian restaurant which I had only visited once and knew I could survive never visiting again. He had never had Indian food before so I had to choose for him. Vindaloo crossed my mind (don't be so cruel).

I had a refresher course on brewing, and eventually we got to the end of our meal. The idea of joining him for a nightcap was raised – and ignored.

All evening he had been clutching a white carrier bag. He now retrieved it from under his chair, and told me he had brought me a couple of presents. He then proceeded to open the bag. First out was a pen stamped with his brewery's name, then came a box of Black Magic followed by a T-shirt bearing a crude suggestion.

As I admired all these gifts, he presented me with a flat cardboard box. The look on his face told me to beware. He was very animated. He urged me to open it and with dread I did. Inside the box were two garments fashioned out of black plastic bin liners and a pair of black stockings. One garment was a low-cut crop top and the other was a mini skirt. He was very excited by now and very red-faced, and he very confidently informed me that he wanted me to wear them later for him. I sat for a moment or two wondering how to extricate myself from this horrendous predicament.

I decided that I needed the loo, and went there clutching the white carrier bag and its contents. Nothing else for it but to try to escape. I came out of the ladies and very carefully sidled round the edges of the restaurant until I came to the door.

I was about to make my escape when a waiter called me back. With sinking heart I turned to see what he wanted and he thrust a red carnation into my hand. I opened the door and fled up the high street with my carrier and carnation flapping in the wind, threw myself into my car and drove home.

The chocolates were white and two years out of date.

I kept my phone on the answerphone for the next week and gradually the calls from him got less and less. When I had not had any for a few days I decided it would be safe to return it to the normal mode. He got through one afternoon when I was least expecting it.

He wanted to see me again. I was a woman with fire and spirit!

Kirsty G., 43, mature student

❦❦❦

Can't be bothered, you say.

You might want to think that, but guess what, your friends, they won't let you. So they make an effort and arrange a date. A date! A blind date? Oh my God. Why bother?

And then you start thinking. Well, maybe this time, you never know. It could be this tall, dark, handsome stranger!

You should know better, but there you are, putting your best, not over-the-top, gear on; getting quite worried about the colour of your hair and wishing you had dieted for the last six months.

The bell rings and the classic, you open the door and look the wrong way – you should have looked down, not up. Never mind, think of Dudley Moore.

Ignore the quilted anorak and cross your fingers, hoping that he is taking you to some exotic place.

Exotic, all right. Greek. The most dingy Greek restaurant in the whole of the North.

You know it's going to be bad when after half an hour, not only has no one else turned up, but it is the wizened old waiter who asks the gentleman if the lady wouldn't like a drink.

The gentleman hasn't a clue as to what to suggest. Can't decide on what to eat either, and has what you order. Where is your knight in shining armour?

None of that. He just talks about problems with his kids. Seems to want a shoulder to cry on.

You want a shoulder to cry on.

God, it's only half past nine? What time can I go home without being rude?

Finally, you're taken home at last.

'Can I see you again?' he says. Cowardly, you reply, 'Maybe.'

Next morning, a big bouquet of flowers with the message 'For a wonderful evening.' Oh dear. Guilt. And you were only being polite.

Patience F., 52, lecturer

🎗🎗🎗

I'd advertised for a warm, caring man. He sounded really nice on the phone. He left a message which implied I was the woman for him. 'Where have you been all my life? I can't wait to meet you,' he said.

I should have seen the warning signs. But no, I thought he would be witty, amusing, attentive – and basically it's nice to be flattered, even if it is a load of old bullshit. He said his name was Des, he was forty-three and a globe-trotting photographer (wonderful, someone with an artistic bent *and* well-travelled).

He insisted that I meet him at a particular underground station because he 'knew a wonderful bar'. (Another warning sign ignored – never agree to go to their old stomping ground!)

The day came, and full of trepidation I drove to the station with my trusted A-Z on my lap. He was fifteen minutes late – another warning sign ignored.

When he arrived I felt somewhat deflated. He looked at least ten years older than he'd told me, and wore a tatty/smelly leather jacket (circa 1973).

The bar was reasonably nice, so I thought I'd have a

quick drink and then make my excuses. But the quick drink was not to be. He began by going into detail about his mother's recent death and being the mug that I am, I felt sorry for him.

He then started to talk about photography. Of course, David Bailey had nothing on him. He was the best, and only took jobs that paid thousands of pounds. By this time I was convinced that the guy was a complete prat. I tried to leave, but he insisted on buying me another drink.

It was then that he decided to show me his portfolio. He pulled out this rather large folder from his briefcase. 'I've made a million twice and spent it twice, I can do it again,' he informed me. He showed me various press cuttings and bank statements going back over twenty years. 'That's when I made my first million,' he said. He then proceeded to tell me how he'd defrauded a leading bank out of three-quarters of a million pounds. 'They can't touch me. I'm too intelligent.'

He went on. And on. And on.

Then came the moment I had been dreading – the photographs. The first batch were fashion/haute couture from catalogues. He'd forgotten to remove the photographer's name, which (surprise surprise) was not his.

As we went through the album, the photographs became what you might call cheap, soft-focus glamour shots and eventually soft porn. 'That's my ex-wife, the supermodel, until drugs ruined her career.'

Oh sure, Des.

And did he really think I would be impressed by photos of young women pouting in various stages of undress? He seemed really pissed off when I said, out of politeness, that they were 'OK' and 'just glamour shots'.

After two-and-a-half hours, I finally said, 'I've got an early start tomorrow, I must go.' He replied, 'I'd love to see you again, you're so attractive and intelligent. I'll call you soon.' I was so relieved I hadn't mentioned that I was changing to cable at the weekend – and would have a new phone number.

So I learned the hard way.

Those little warning signs should NEVER be ignored . . .

Lorraine A., 32, teacher

🍷🍷🍷

I met Eddie at a club on one of those drunken nights . . . The ones where you're trying to forget all your worries, and how you could happily rearrange your ex-boyfriend's face for two-timing you with Sharon-from-down-the-road.

My vodka-drenched memories of Eddie remained those of a faceless man snogging me in one corner of the dance floor, and I was therefore surprised to receive a phone call inviting me to lunch. Obviously, I'd been enough in control to give Eddie my number – so I agreed. It was better than waiting for a bus to come and land on Sharon-from-down-the-road's head.

My friend Lyn was no help in describing Eddie, although she did remember me talking to a mature-

looking guy who went on about his BMW in great
detail. Only thing was, when she said 'mature', I
didn't realize she meant 'maturing to a ripe old age'.
Opening the door to Eddie was like greeting one of
the gnomes who sat at the bottom of my back garden
– at least a thirty-year-old one at that! Even so,
height did not account for his attire: I'll swear he
was auditioning for a part in *Joseph and the
Technicolour Dreamcoat*. His shirt bore every colour
under the sun, and even they could not match his
baggy corduroy trousers.

I closed my eyes and thought of his BMW. But I was
in for another disappointment. Sitting in the driveway
was a bright red Volkswagen Beetle. You couldn't miss
it; it would have doubled for a traffic light.

A big mistake, asking why he'd borrowed a friend's
car. It would seem men with multi-coloured shirts are
maniac mechanics. Eddie went from his gearstick right
through to his crankshaft. I prayed that bus would come
and land on my head instead.

Romantic luncheon notions were also cast aside as
we pulled up at The Dog and Beetle pub. Eddie charged
in and ordered beer and food for us both: it clearly
wasn't a 'ladies' choice' pub. He also appeared to know
the barman and the majority of the football louts
lounging along the bar. They made some lewd
comments, as only football fans seem able to do. I smiled
sweetly as I turned to concentrate on my chips – they
looked like being my only company for the next two
hours.

Enough was enough, though, and when my stomach
began to feel queasy, I demanded to leave. My burger

had obviously contained something as intolerable as the occupants of the pub.

However, we'd not driven more than two turns down the back roads we'd arrived by, when the car bumped, jerked and veered into a bush. Amidst a barrage of swearing Eddie announced a flat tyre. Then he looked at me in that funny way that men do and suddenly reappeared on my side of the car.

My stomach churned again and I told Eddie in no uncertain terms to 'sort it out'. (If that was a flat tyre, I was Sharon-from-down-the-road.)

Clearly the guy did not get the message. The next thing I knew, my door flew open and there stood Eddie, modelling nothing but his Donald Duck boxers.

My stomach could take no more and I promptly deposited the remnants of my lunch at Eddie's feet.

I never was a great lover of Donald Duck.

Lisa M., 19, student

🐾🐾🐾

There was just the one thing that my mother couldn't understand – that I was twenty-four years old and not married. This, what's more, despite her leaning towards erudition, which she'd tried to pass on to me. It was an impulse so powerful in her that it would cause her to bring the weekly philosophy society meetings to an untimely end – typically, by shouting out during some unfortunate fellow's closing speech that it was Kant not Schopenhauer who had developed the Categorical

Imperative. This had the effect of making the poor chap look very stupid. This was one of her favourite pastimes, making men look foolish.

Unfortunately, however, she was unable to make any connection between her behaviour and my inability or lack of desire to find a suitable spouse. So she was constantly on the hunt for suitable husband material for me.

Every Tuesday night she went to play a mysterious East European card game at the house of a friend who took in lodgers. That particular Tuesday, the friend mentioned to my mother that she had a new lodger, one Bernard, who was on the lookout for a partner too.

My mother, never one to miss a trick, in either cards or life, leapt upon this opportunity and promised to arrange a date. The following morning I appeared for breakfast to be greeted by my mother, saying 'I hef arranged a date for you mit Bernard. You wil go, jah!' Just this once, I dutifully clicked my heels, raised my arm in that well-known salute and replied, 'Jahwohl, mein Fuhrer.'

Bernard was a stolid chap, dressed in a brownish suit from Man at Burton.

It totally reflected his personality.

He was slightly bald and, for me, ever so slightly boring. To offset this, however, he had turned up in a sports car. This he dutifully drove at a speed of about 27.5 m.p.h.

I'd wanted to go to the local Indian which served curry without cutlery, you used your hands and a chapatti. Bernard preferred a nearby restaurant run by a very nice Greek family, whose speciality was that well-known Greek dish, Chicken Kiev.

Bernard was studying engineering. My knowledge in this area was almost nil, so I asked him to explain all about it. An hour-and-a-half later, I really was none the wiser.

The meal was over and as we were driving back, I suddenly had a vision of life at forty, me in a mink jacket staring gloomily out of the window of a Volvo Estate with a chubbier, older, balder Bernard sitting next to me. I broke into a cold sweat and, promptly pleading a headache (which was wiser than confessing to hallucinations), asked Bernard to take me home.

I nipped smartly out of the car, heading off a pass at the pass. I had other things on my mind. In particular, avoiding a KGB interrogation from Mrs Joe Stalin. No such luck! She was there, waiting for me as I opened the front door.

'Vell, so I suppose as usual you messed up. You behaved badly und now ze whole town vill know.'

'But, but . . .' I stuttered.

'Vy do I bother, all ze money spent on your education – ein complete waste, und so I don't speak viz you again.'

With that, she stormed off and, true to her word, didn't speak to me for a week. However, after returning from cards the following Tuesday, she sailed in through the front door and hugged me fervently as if nothing was amiss.

'*Daalink*, I'm so proud von you. They told me Bernard had a wonderful time und he likes you very much. Of course, I always knew you vouldn't let me down. So, you see him again, ja?'

'Maybe,' I said, 'let's talk later.'

I slunk off quietly to bed, relieved that for that day at least, the war was over.

Natalie R., 38, insurance company receptionist

4

'Noooo . . .':
Humiliation

He was tall, with dark brown hair, deeply penetrating eyes and a slightly twisted smile that gave him the blasé expression of a man who had been there before . . . many times. So why he should choose me from the long line of exotic wallflowers elegantly draping the fringes of the nightclub disco both mystified and delighted me.

Linda, my companion of many Saturday nights, looked amazed too. She usually took me along to draw a sharp distinction between her graceful, long-legged blonde looks and my 5-foot, comfortable 10 stone. I knew she didn't really like me but I didn't care; sometimes it pays to be in the company of a beautiful blonde . . . as it did tonight.

While we danced I felt him scrutinizing me. Had that wretched spot on my nose resurrected itself? I wondered with dread. Maybe he was just the strong, silent type.

'Next you're going to ask me if I come here often!' I quipped, but the joke fell horribly flat.

'Shall we retire to the bar?' he said when the dance ended.

I tried to prop myself on the bar stool in what I believed to be a sophisticated pose.

'What do you normally drink?' he asked.

'I don't . . . well, not often . . . I'll have a Coke,' I ended lamely. As we sipped our drinks and he continued his steady gaze I knew that I should have ordered a double brandy; the situation certainly called for a stimulant.

'Do you mind if I ask your age?' he said, piercing my nervousness with those compelling eyes of his.

'Twenty-three,' I replied, being a firm believer in poetic licence.

'And what are your hobbies?'

I hesitated. What do you say to a man who looks as if he has been round the world several times?

'Reading,' I suggested tentatively. That could possibly cover a wide field.

'And do you like sport?'

'Love watching football . . . and cricket,' I said with more enthusiasm, omitting to mention that I only ever watched from a television ringside seat. This line of conversation could lead to more exciting things, perhaps. He certainly appeared interested as he fumbled in his inner pocket. My dreams soared.

He's searching for his diary, I told myself in a state of bliss, suddenly visualizing those innumerable Saturday nights with Linda converted into idyllic evenings by a village cricket pitch.

To my amazement he produced an envelope from which he extracted a printed form.

'Have you in the past, or would you in the future ever consider using a dating agency?' he enquired, perusing his notes.

I might if the end result was someone like you, I thought.

Aloud I asked him, 'What is this all about?'

'Just a few more questions,' he replied patiently.

'In aid of what exactly?' My voice was adopting a more strident note all on its own.

'Market research for ****** Introduction Services,' he replied, without bothering to look up. 'Here's my card.'

Noooo . . .

I gave the slip of cardboard the sort of attention he had so far afforded me.

'Now finally, could you tell me whether you consider yourself:

a) Lonely

b) Friendly, but in need of male company

c) Interesting to be with

d) Shy but a good conversationalist when drawn out?'

I dropped the business card into his glass of whisky and rose to my full 5 foot.

'A loser,' I said, and stalked out of the bar in search of Linda.

Gina L., 37, personal assistant

🎕🎕🎕

It was our third date. I really liked him. I had actually heard that he was a womanizer, but I thought – no no, he won't be like that with me. He invited me to dinner at his place. When I arrived, his flatmate was there, and another woman.

I discovered I was expected to cook. 'Thanks, darling,' he said. 'Whenever I do it it tastes disgusting.' I thought

81

this was a bit much. But then, well, I *was* his girlfriend . . .

So I went into the kitchen, and started to prepare the food. The kitchen door was open, and I happened to look round. There was my so-called boyfriend, doing some heavy necking with the other woman.

I finished the cooking, put the meat and vegetables and rice on the table, and walked out.

As I shut the door, I thought – I hope they enjoy the rice.

I'd cooked it to perfection in lightly salted water and six large squirts of Fairy Liquid.

Jennifer M., 33, manager

🌸🌸🌸

I was seventeen years old, and I had just started my first job at the bank. Dick was the office hunk. At nineteen, he was the best-looking guy I had ever seen in my life. He helped me settle in, and within a few weeks I had fallen head over heels for him.

All the other young girls of my age fancied him too, so I knew I stood no chance with him. You can imagine my surprise when, after working with him for three months, he very casually asked 'Well, Francesca, how about coming to see *The Empire Strikes Back* with me tonight?'

My dreams had been answered. I was so excited I thought my heart would burst. He took my address and arranged to pick me up at seven that night.

He looked even more handsome out of his suit. In jeans, he was the sexiest man alive. He was friendly and polite to my parents, reassuring them that he'd bring me home by eleven-thirty.

I watched with pride as he opened the door of his new low-slung sports car for me. Suddenly a voice shouted, 'Hello, are you my bruvver's new girlfriend?' I looked in horror at the scruffy little eleven-year-old sitting in the back.

'Oh Francesca, this is Brian my brother. I got lumbered with baby-sitting. He'll be no trouble. He's been dying to see the film too.'

In an instant my bubble burst. I'd spent three months dreaming for a moment like this to happen, and now that it had I was completely shattered.

Once at the cinema, Dick paid for himself and his brother, leaving me to pay for myself.

Brian sat between us, stuffing himself with chocolates and popcorn, throughout the whole two hours.

After the film Dick and his brother bought saveloy and chips. Suddenly I saw Dick in an even worse light – he just *wolfed* down his food.

The absolute worst part was the journey home. Dick actually had the cheek to ask me for 'petrol money', seeing as he had come out to collect me and drive me home.

I was just about to complain when his 'adorable' little brother was sick all over my right shoulder.

I stormed out of the car, and out of Dick's life, for ever. His dating life, anyway. The next day at work he very casually said to me, 'Hey, it was a good night last night, Francesca. We'll have to do it again sometime.'

The funny thing is . . . he wasn't joking either.
                                    Francesca P., 31, bank teller

🍃🍃🍃

He was drop-dead gorgeous. A fabulous specimen. So many muscles. His biceps looked like sackfuls of fighting hedgehogs.

'Let's go out to play on Saturday,' he said.

Our first date!

I could hardly speak for excitement.

He was going to pick me up at twelve. I spent three hours bathing, wrestling with unwanted body hair, making up, scenting, trying on ten combinations of sexy T-shirts and sparkly leggings.

He rolled up and tooted his horn. 'Oh,' I thought. 'Bit rude.'

He leaned across to open the car door for me. 'Sorry I didn't get out of the car, Rache,' he said. 'I haven't told you – but I've injured my leg playing rugby.' He then launched into a discussion of tendons that, in length and detail, could have graced any medical textbook. I started to feel a bit queasy.

'There's somewhere I've just got to go first,' he said. He stopped outside a very swish Regency terraced house. 'Ooh,' I thought, 'I'm to meet his friends already!'

Er, no. His physiotherapist.

'I'll only be half an hour,' he said. 'Would you mind waiting?'

I sat down on a worn and slightly slashed leather

settee and buried myself in a palaeolithic copy of *Country Life*.

I was not a happy bunny. But still, those muscles.

After three-quarters of an hour, out he came.

'She recommends I start exercising it now,' he said.

When he said now, he meant now. Our next stop was his gym.

'There's a canteen if you're hungry,' he said. 'Then perhaps you'd like to come and watch?'

One carrot juice and a wholewheat bun that tasted of ferret droppings later, I walked down to the gym. There was superhunk, a-heaving and a-stretching, fine body a-sheen with honest sweat.

'Oh hi,' he said. 'Won't be long now.'

Half an hour later, he said, 'Right, that's it.' He went to shower and change. I could feel my teeth starting involuntarily to grind.

'Never mind,' I said to myself. 'Be fair. He *is* injured.'

'Let's go back to my place,' he said.

Ah ha.

When we got to his flat, he suggested we watch a video. Not quite what I had in mind for a Saturday afternoon, but never mind. Perhaps it would be a sexy, romantic prelude to get us in the mood for the rest of the day . . .

It was an England/Wales rugby match.

I sat, catatonic with fury.

When it was over, he said, 'Let's go out to dinner.'

'I'm sorry,' I said, leaping to my feet. 'I've suddenly developed a bad ache in my insides. I'm off. Do take enormous, terrific care of your body, won't you.'

Rachel M., 27, TV researcher

He was my teacher at my weekly evening class, and I really really fancied him. I thought what the hell, and rang him to ask him out for a drink. We arranged that I'd pick him up outside the bus station on Sunday evening. He was late, I was hysterical with nerves, and he was already drunk from beer at lunchtime. We just sat in this horrible, tense silence in the car.

I'd once said in class that I wanted to get married. When we got to the pub, his opening gambit was to ask me why I thought marriage was such a good institution. So within ten minutes of sitting down, he was telling me about how he never wanted to get married, he didn't want that sort of commitment, being tied to one woman, etc. etc. etc. When he'd finished making himself blindingly clear on that score, we moved on to funerals and death.

Both of us were getting drunker and drunker.

Finally he told me he was leaving, and I said wouldn't he like to stay for a while and go somewhere else. 'It's not that I don't find you attractive,' he said, 'but I'm going home now.'

When we got outside, I started trying to snog him and he wouldn't snog me back, and he was so tall, and I was craning upwards and he wasn't bending downwards . . .

I shall never ever go back to my evening class. I'd rather be bitten to death by crocodiles – at least it might be a bit more dignified.

Helen P., 29, writer

❦❦❦

Things had not been going too well between Dave and me, and I suspected he just might have been seeing someone else. However, he was still declaring his undying love at every opportunity. So I decided, with Valentine's Day approaching, that I would pull out all the stops and try to win him back completely. I booked the restaurant, complete with rose which I had decided to ask the waitress to present to him (just to keep things equal).

I arrived at his house ten minutes early, trying to contain my excitement at the anticipated thrill awaiting us. He eventually arrived home half an hour late, making some excuse about being held up in traffic. However, undaunted and determined that nothing would spoil the romantic evening I had planned, off we went.

When we arrived the waitress came over and duly delivered the rose as requested. He looked quite touched, if not a little embarrassed, at the gesture. But I had already decided, why should flowers be exclusively for women? I may even start a new trend.

It was then I noticed it.

Surely not, I thought.

It must be the lighting.

No, it was definitely . . .

Like a reflex action my hand moved his head to one side and yes, it definitely was!

'What is that on your neck?' I demanded.

'Oh that,' he said, and as he said it I'm sure I noticed

a self-satisfied smirk creep over his face.

'Do your shirt up at once,' I said, horrified. 'The waitress will think that I did it,' realizing I was at the point of no return on my evening out and trying to salvage my pride.

Our meal arrived, although my ravenous appetite had changed to nagging nausea. But I picked my way through it, still determined not to spoil the evening I had spent weeks mentally preparing for, so I tried to change the subject. (I have always had a fairly persistent stubborn streak.)

He definitely did not want to make small talk. Well, as luck would have it, a large video screen came down from the ceiling in front of us and Michael Jackson started to gyrate and crotch rub, creating the perfect escape from any kind of confrontational conversation that might have ensued.

When we had finished eating, I suggested we could go downstairs and dance. Only if his favourite record came on, he replied, and of course it didn't. 'How about another drink?' I asked, trying not to sound too domineering. 'No, I don't think so,' came the reply. Having just devoured a large meal and a complete bottle of champagne, while I sipped mineral water, he was looking rather sleepy. 'I think I'm about ready to go home,' he announced.

Now I like to think I'm no quitter, but I was certainly being tested to the limit. Keep smiling, I thought, it may just be a bad dream and I might wake up any minute.

Just to complete my evening, he fell asleep in the car on the way home. The journey took three-quarters of an hour. It seemed a lot longer. When we arrived, he stirred just enough to mutter, "Bye' and staggered indoors. "BYE DAVE, DON'T CALL ME . . .'

Trish N., 35, district nurse

🍂🍂🍂

During my second year at university I became attracted to a student from my class called Martin. He was considered a very good catch, so I could hardly believe my luck when he finally asked me out.

Thereafter, the luck ran out . . . He cancelled the date on three occasions, always at the last minute and always for rather dubious excuses.

We arranged to meet a fourth time. *He turned up*. Fifteen minutes late, but he was there. Oh joy.

We had a quiet drink, and then Martin decided it would be fun to go to a nightclub. When we arrived he asked me what I'd like to drink and made his way to the bar. In no time he rushed back looking quite flustered. I asked him if anything was wrong, to which he replied 'See that girl serving behind the bar? I stood her up on Friday . . . so would you mind going to get the drinks?'

Clare T., 25, personnel officer

🍂🍂🍂

89

I'd met Roger in one of our local pubs on a Saturday night. You know the sort of guy – confident and charming, tall, dark, smouldering eyes. Got the picture?

He told me he had just started working as an accountant for a large firm. I was thrilled when he asked me out. He promised to call the next day; that I took with a pinch of salt.

Well, his promise came true; he rang the following afternoon. We chatted for nearly an hour and arranged to see a movie on Tuesday evening. Roger said he'd pick me up in his car.

Tuesday arrived. As I walked in from work the phone rang. It was Roger, explaining that his car had broken down. He asked if I would pick him up instead.

That was quite reasonable, I thought. I arranged to pick him up at eight p.m. at the end of his road. I drove up, fashionably late.

'Aaah,' I thought, as he stood there looking gorgeous.

We drove straight to the cinema. At the kiosk Roger told me that he had forgotten his wallet and asked if I could pay. 'Great,' I thought, likely story. However, like a mug I paid. I also paid for the popcorn, Coke and chocolate raisins. Roger had quite an appetite.

After the film we popped next door to the pub for last orders. At the bar we bumped into Roger's sister. I had to include her in the round too, it would have been rude not to.

Roger's sister explained that she had run out of money. Obviously it ran in the family.

She asked Roger if she could borrow £10, and when he explained that he too didn't have any on him, she asked me. I was so gobsmacked – I had only just met her, for goodness' sake. In my surprise I said 'yes,' and handed over a hard-earned tenner.

As if that wasn't enough she asked me for a lift home.

But then I looked at Roger and he smiled down at me with those smouldering eyes – my heart decided for me . . .

After dropping off the sister from hell, I took Roger home and he invited me in for coffee. I thought it would be nice – after all we had hardly had half an hour to ourselves, what with the film and his sister. We went up to his flat, which turned out to be a bedroom with a shared bathroom above a shop. Strange, I thought, for a chartered accountant. Roger then confessed that er, actually, he was a student.

He proceeded to bring in the coffee, fetch his PJs, go into the bathroom, get changed, come back and climb into bed. I sat there absolutely amazed. Would he like me to fetch his teddy bear? Read him a bedtime story? He leaned forward, kissed me on the cheek and asked me to shut the shop door firmly behind me.

To add insult to injury, it took me two months to get my £10 back from his sister.

Maria B., 30, television production assistant

Phil and I had been writing for nearly a year, since his return to South Africa. We had been lovers until he lost his job and had to leave the country. Originally he had planned to return a couple of months later, but was offered such a good deal that he decided to stay in Cape Town.

I missed him, and wrote to say I would like to come to visit. He seemed keen, and suggested December or January. I emptied my savings account, booked my ticket and wrote with flight details.

One month later I still hadn't received a reply. I wrote again.

Three days before my departure I received a call from his sister in England, telling me Phil had faxed her to confirm my arrangements. He would meet me at the airport, and could I bring over some Nike trainers and duty-free perfume (for his mother, I assumed). I was so relieved and happy. We would be together for Christmas!

I spent hours in the aeroplane loo, preening.

As I strolled through the arrivals hall there he was, smiling, with outstretched arms. As we drove down the highway he explained that I would be staying with him and Elizabeth. 'We're just friends sharing a place,' he reassured me.

We entered the apartment. Beautifully furnished and welcoming. As I wandered round, I realized.

Only one bedroom.

'Don't worry,' he told me kindly. 'We've got a mattress for you to sleep on on the floor.'

Sandy Y., 29, bar manager

🐾🐾🐾

Picture the scene. It was a snowy, romantic night –
New Year's Eve – and I was heading off for a fancy
dress (or so I thought) party with some people I was
living with. I was to meet my hot date for the night:
Dermot, one of an Irish family who ran a country pub
in a little village some miles away.

I'd had my eye on him for a while because he was
stunningly good-looking and certainly had a lot of
Irish charm. I was totally under his spell and he'd
certainly cast it well over me, having promised me a
romantic night to celebrate the New Year. So, dressed
only in a flimsy 1920s-style dress, feather boa and
pearls, I went.

When we got there (me flushed with excitement),
it was to find that the small bar was crammed with
Hell's Angels who were certainly *not* in fancy dress
– well, no more than usual anyway – and who were
looking decidedly unfestive. It was stiflingly hot and
because it had taken us so long to get there through
the snow, the party was already – shall we say –
lively. Dermot seemed pleased to see me, however.
At first. But things slid rapidly downhill from there
on in.

I soon found out that I was one of five women who
thought they were there on a date with him that night.
At one stage I actually caught him with his hand down
the front of a woman's dress in the ladies' loo! But before
that, he'd carried on dispensing the old charm to me at
regular intervals, keeping me interested, and presumably everyone else as well . . .

Shortly after the loo debacle, a huge fight broke out
just on the stroke of midnight. I spent what had been

billed as a 'romantic moment' squashing myself around the side of the bar to avoid being hit by broken glass, and being shouted at unceremoniously by Dermot to 'get back round the other side' – that was, directly into the fray. My dress got torn, God knows where the feather boa went and we all ended up out on the pavement where the snow lay deep and crisp and even – and absolutely freezing. My knight in shining armour, meanwhile, was cowering behind the relative safety of the bar.

To cap it all, when the police had gone, he decided to spend a romantic moment with me – and asked me to help him wash up the glasses as the machine had broken down! Not surprisingly I declined.

To end the 'perfect' evening, the person I'd travelled with had disappeared upstairs with one of Dermot's sisters and I was stranded twenty miles from home at one-thirty a.m. on New Year's Day. But I was determined that I was going to go home despite Dermot's protestations that I could share his bed!

Madness overtook me and with the rashness of youth, I took my debauched friend's car keys out of his jacket and drove his brand new BMW home, uninsured, through the snow and along treacherously icy country lanes. Being in a total rage at this stage, I naturally couldn't find the heater and practically died of hypothermia on the way home.

My New Year's resolution – no more 'dates' with Dermot – I had *no* trouble keeping.

Diane H., 29, press officer

❦❦❦

As a teenager, my success with boys was virtually non-existent. I was rather thin, with short straight hair that defied any attempt to curl it, and I disliked wearing make-up except for mascara and lip-gloss. My gamin looks did little to attract the opposite sex, who seemed to prefer my more glamorous and decorative friends. But although sometimes I thought it would be nice to have a boyfriend like the other girls at college, at nineteen I was really more interested in getting my History and Arts degree. After all, I reasoned, there would be plenty of time for boys later.

Then one evening at the weekly college disco, my luck seemed to change. An absolutely gorgeous man kept staring in my direction. I knew most of the boys who came regularly to the discos, but I'd never seen this one before. He looked in his early twenties, tall and slim, with shining hair and dark eyes.

For a long time he didn't approach me, but I could sense his eyes watching me intently. I felt embarrassed – but interested, and kept wishing I had worn a dress instead of my habitual jeans and loose sweater. I danced continually to cover my nervousness, then suddenly as I turned round, he was there – there on the dance floor right in front of me. He didn't speak, but a faint smile on his lips tried to reassure me as we moved together to the heavy beat of the band.

When the music stopped he followed me to my table and sat down. He introduced himself as Stephen. He worked in an antique shop, and loved historical artefacts and *objets d'art* – we had so much in common it seemed too good to be true.

We talked and talked into the late hours. My self-consciousness disappeared and I felt completely at ease with him. It was as if we'd known each other all our lives.

He hadn't flirted with me or tried to make a pass all evening, except to hold my hand. But when it was about twelve o'clock and he suggested going back to my room for coffee, I found myself agreeing with him. Male visitors were not allowed in our rooms, but somehow or other it could usually be arranged. The two other girls who shared with me had gone home for the weekend so I knew that Stephen and I wouldn't be disturbed.

I guessed that there was more than coffee on his mind, and as soon as we were alone, he took me in his arms. He was so gentle – kissing and caressing my face and neck, and holding me close to him. I was completely under his spell. Slowly, he led me to the bed and we lay down, still kissing and stroking each other. As his hand glided gently over my stomach, he gave a mild look of surprise. Then his fingers started to move under and upwards beneath my sweater.

Suddenly he jumped back in alarm and pushed me away. 'Good grief!' he exclaimed. 'You're a g-g-girl!'

Tricia Y., 27, housewife and mother

❧❧❧

He must have been one of the sexiest men I'd ever dated. It was attraction at first sight, and after a hot night together I was very optimistic about him. Finally, a perfect boyfriend, I thought. Is it going to work out now?

I was on the way to our second date, and gave the final touch to my make-up in the back seat of a taxi. After all the painstaking hours I'd spent finding the right clothes to wear I simply had to look gorgeous now . . .

He was waiting for me in the bar, a glass of mineral water in his hand. Oh, what a man, he doesn't even drink, I thought, and his value in my eyes rose even more.

I had no idea how long we had been sitting there at a remote table, holding each other's hands and exchanging deep glances. It seemed like I was falling in love again after such a long time, and that finally Mr Right had come my way. Happiness made me feel dizzy. I pressed his hand and he responded to me. Even without words, we seemed to understand each other completely. 'I've got to tell you something,' he said with a charming smile. 'I've had girls before you . . .'

'It's OK, it's perfectly OK.' I felt like melting into his eyes. 'It doesn't disturb me . . .'

'And there's a certain thing they all have done for me . . . Something special, you know.'

'Oh, I see.' In my mind, I imagined all the spicy details of our lovemaking that a man like him, so stylish, so original, could desire . . . Probably something like a champagne bath and underwear in purple silk . . .

Or maybe a date somewhere in the city, when I'd wear nothing but stockings under my coat and we'd have sex on the top floor of a double-decker as it drove through the neon-lit streets . . .

'You think you could cope with it?' he wondered.

'Whatever it is, it turns me on,' I whispered to him.

'OK then,' he said. 'My rent and phone bill, you know . . . can you pay them for this month and the next one?'

Roxanne D., 21, currently unemployed

❦❦❦

I thought Hugh was utterly yummy scrummy. Blond hair, azure eyes, Y-shaped figure, Hugo Boss jackets. He was a friend of my (also very beautiful) flatmate Sarah.

He used to drop round quite a lot. The more I got to know him, the more I'd got to like him. And because he often came unexpectedly, he'd seen me at my worst. In ancient, manky Marks & Sparks flannel dressing gown, hair in scarecrow mode where I'd been sleeping on it, make-up-less.

One day when Sarah was away on a week's course, Hugh came round and for once I looked decent. I was going to a dinner party later, and I was made up, combed, and kitted out in my best French Connection. 'You look lovely, Caroline,' he said.

I was so thrilled my toes curled.

We chatted away over coffee, and suddenly he said,

'I wonder if you'd fancy having dinner with me tomorrow night?'

Is the Pope a Catholic?

Does the earth go round the sun?

Is my stomach holding the Butterflies' Ball?

'Ooh, yes please,' I squeaked.

Not terribly cool, I thought. Get a grip, for God's sake.

'That would be very kind,' I said, slightly more calmly.

The next day I took a two-and-a-half hour lunch-break.

I scoured the designer shops in Knightsbridge. I had never had a designer outfit in my life. Finally, I found The Dress. If I say so myself, I looked pretty damned fine – and so I should, at that price.

Nearly a month's salary.

I would have to visit my bank manager, crawl along the carpet and lick his brogues.

After the least productive afternoon of my entire career, I dashed home. The rush-hour tube seemed crammed with the most attractive people I'd seen in my life. Even the rats running along the rails looked cute.

I parked myself in the bathroom, and did every conceivably beautifying thing to every bit of my body that I could think of. My hands were trembling so much I nearly poked my eye out with my mascara wand. I kept bursting out in a sweat and having to rewash my armpits.

Finally, I slithered into The Dress. I looked at myself in the wardrobe mirror; and I was satisfied.

He'd seen me looking awful, and had still asked me out. So if this didn't slay him, nothing would.

He came to pick me up on the dot of seven-thirty, in his totally stylish car. I mean, as you'd expect.

In the car I found myself planning the wedding. I just couldn't help it. My imagination took on a fiendishly uncontrollable life of its own. Sarah as bridesmaid, of course, for playing matchmaker. My mother on tranquillizers, she gets so overcome at weddings. Did Hugo Boss do women's bridal wear? And I did hope our babies would have his heart-stopping eyes . . .

We arrived at a very sophisticated restaurant. I sailed in, for once full of confidence. I looked good and I was with the most gorgeous man in London.

We sat down, chatted through the starter – I was so whipped up I could only swallow a mouthful of lettuce. As we waited for the main course, he suddenly looked a bit shy.

How *sweet*, I thought.

'Caroline,' he said.

'Yes Hugh,' I said, encouragingly.

'I know I might look confident.'

Oh you do, you do, I thought . . .

'But actually I'm very shy when it comes to women. And when I'm really in love, I seem to become totally paralysed. I just can't say what I want to say, and I'm so afraid of rejection.'

I nearly swooned on the spot. Could this really be happening to me? Do dreams come true after all?

'Oh Hugh,' I gasped. 'There's no chance of you being rejected.'

His face lit up.
'Oh Caroline. Do you think Sarah likes me then?'

Caroline R., 29, researcher

5
'I just wanted to vanish':
Embarrassment

He was absolutely the most divine, scrumptious, handsome man I'd ever seen. I'm a doctor's receptionist, and one day he'd walked in to register as a new arrival in the area, and asked me out. He booked dinner at eight p.m. on Saturday at a seriously mega-posh restaurant. Was I thrilled. My idea of a big night out is an American Hot and a couple of breadsticks at the local Pizza Hut.

As soon as we walked in my spine went quite cold. It was the twilight zone. All the customers looked just like my bank manager. We sat down at a table covered with cutlery, perfect white serviettes shaped like cones and a frightening number of glasses.

Over the first glass of wine I started to relax a bit. Robert was just so wonderful. He was charming, and funny, and actually *asked me questions about myself*. I don't normally get that sort of treatment. He said 'one does' and 'one feels' a lot, but I reckoned I could get used to it. Oh, could I be this lucky . . .?

At that moment, the waiter snatched up my serviette. I automatically made to snatch it back. He gave me a blood-freezing look, shook it out and placed it over my lap.

Oops.

'What would you like to begin with, Sally? Oh, nothing?' Robert said. 'Well, for a main course, they do a very succulent seafood platter.'

'Um fine,' I said. 'Whatever you think.'

If he'd suggested a pile of nails garnished with gerbil droppings in a spot of gnat's piss I'd have said yes, frankly. When you think this might be Mr Right at last you have to nod a lot, that's my theory.

Scampi and chips are really as far as I've gone in the seafood department. When I saw the bit of log covered with shells, eyes, tentacles and small rubbery lumps I could feel myself starting to panic.

By the time I'd put a long metal skewer the wrong way up a bit of lobster, couldn't manage to yank a prawn out of its shell and struggled with a snail, Robert took pity on me and did a lot of winkling and shell cracking. And then I could hardly get the disgusting stuff down me.

I thought: he must think I'm so hopeless, I've got to try to *entertain* him somehow. A joke, that was it. I could only remember the start of one – all I could think was that it had given me a big laugh at the time. So I thought if I begin, I expect the rest will come back to me. It was a really long shaggy dog story about a Corsican peasant. As I got near the end, I remembered the punchline. It was about having sex with – with – a goat. Oh my *God*. Why did I have to remember that one? Robert was smiling in anticipation. My brain went completely numb. I said 'Oh, oh, Robert, you won't believe this, I've forgotten the punchline, ha ha.'

'Never mind, Sally,' he said. But I saw the way his eyebrows twitched.

Pudding was profiteroles, my absolute favourite. Just as Robert turned away to summon a waiter for some mineral water, I sliced my spoon into a profiterole, and a blob of cream shot out and landed on my front. I wiped at it hurriedly with my serviette. Robert hadn't yet noticed. Think of something to distract him, quick, quick. I knew Robert worked in the City. City – money – politics . . . But didn't the City like the government? Couldn't remember . . . no time . . .

'Don't you think that last budget was totally hopeless?' I blurted out.

'Actually no, Sally. There are some aspects that should really boost . . .'

I bent my head to hide the tears I could feel just starting to spurt. It was then that I got my first good look at the greasy cream stain on the front of my dress. It was the size of the Mediterranean.

Robert paid the bill and we left. 'I'll find a taxi for you, Sally,' he said. 'It's been, er, great.'

He must've been very healthy. At least, he never came to see the doctor. Ever.

Sally S., 27, doctor's receptionist

❧❧❧

I'd fancied this man at work for ages. We kept bumping into each other by the photocopier, it was thrilling. Finally, he asked me out – to go ten-pin bowling.

The big night arrived. I was nervous as a cat, my palms greasy with sweat. I picked up the ball, ran forward, swung my arm back... The ball shot backwards like a missile, catching the man of my dreams squarely in the most delicate part of his anatomy.

I just wanted to vanish.

Now I have to get someone else to do the photo-copying.

Barbara J., 26, personal assistant

🐾🐾🐾

Fancying herself as the perfect matchmaker, my mother arranged for me to attend my cousin's wedding with a 'charming chap' from her boyfriend's office.

Already this guy had a number of points against him.

Firstly, if he was a friend of Rod's (mother's beau) he was a nerd, as was Rod. Simple deduction. Secondly, the partner I wanted to take was away running some marathon through Africa (what a man!), and thirdly I'd never liked my cousin anyway so I wouldn't have minded not going at all. Oh, it was all so frustrating and the doomed event was scheduled to begin the next evening.

At last the church ceremony was thankfully over. But at least in church you don't have to talk to the person next to you, chatting in pews not going down too well. After we were all seated at the reception, however, there was nothing to save me.

My 'partner' was, let's say, well-groomed, polite, a truly 'charming chap' – all smiles and forever nodding

106

in agreement. The kind of guy who would wash his hands after every handshake.

As the reception wore on, 'partner' began to relax. He munched his way through three plates of dinner, washing them down with bottle after bottle of wine. This was much to the horror of the catering staff, who obviously had not counted on a ravenous lunatic. They were not to know that, on being invited to the wedding a week ago, he had begun fasting.

Disappearing every three minutes, I managed to busy myself with tying cans to the back of the newly-weds' car, helping the kitchen staff wash the dishes and talking earnestly to relatives whom I never knew existed. Exciting stuff, I can tell you.

The crowning glory of the evening was when the music began and 'partner' felt the urge to dance – like a man possessed. He gave new meaning to the word dance; everyone agreed that what he was doing looked utterly painful: a combination of a Latin American salsa/Zulu traditional tribal dance plus some kind of major fit, all to the sounds of Chris de Burgh's 'Lady in Red'.

I have no idea how it ended. Leaving Mother a quickly scribbled note, I hopped in a cab and headed home.

That was five years ago, and I still go beet red thinking about it. To this day I hope no one remembers that it was me who walked through those reception party doors with Him on my arm.

Sonia U., 23, temporary secretary

❧❧❧

It did not start out as a date. I was invited to tea by a married friend who must have decided to play matchmaker. On my arrival, I noticed with alarm that I was not the only visitor. An individual, to whose face I had taken an instant dislike, leered at me with the air of someone who has just made a purchase and was now admiring the goods. I was puzzled by his presence, being a bit slow in certain matters. After a while the penny dropped. I tried to behave like the civilized person I am, forcing myself to overcome my antipathy.

It was not easy.

He talked. And how. He talked about his worldly goods with pride. It seemed he had lots of them. He told us about his latest acquisitions in the line of kitchenware, bed linen, real estate, electrical goods, bulk groceries, medical supplies and so on. Next the talk drifted to his sainted mother, and the great esteem he held her in. We discussed his interesting emotional life, his healthy bank account, his car. My head was spinning.

If he showed signs of slowing down, my so-called friend would urge him on to renewed efforts. After an hour passed in this pleasant manner, I believed I could decently excuse myself and leave. He was out of his seat like a shot. He got hold of my coat and dragged me out from behind the table where I was sitting. He just about came up to my shoulders.

What can he want? I wondered in disbelief as we traipsed down the road. He told me he was going to walk me home. 'There's no need,' I protested weakly. But he was masterful. As he walked through the streets I tried to lengthen my steps. It did not make any difference, he began to run beside me. I was getting agitated. There was an ominous threat in the air.

He then made his move.

He asked me to marry him.

I wiped my forehead in a daze. I was stunned and embarrassed. What should I do? I could tell him I was already married with four children, or that I was just going to enter a nunnery – taking the veil after long consideration – or push him into the garden of the house we were just passing and make a run for it.

I did none of these things. Instead I told him I had no intention of getting married. He wanted to know why, and proceeded to give me a lecture on the advantages and importance of marriage. We returned to his saintly mother again. He dwelt warmly on her long and happy married life, which was an example to him and the reason for his present offer to me, as he wished to emulate this esteemed parent.

But who can he be? I wondered, dumbfounded. I had not caught his name, and why had he picked on me?

When he saw that he wasn't making much impression, he turned to certain delicate matters. In a low, confidential voice, he told me he knew all about me, as he had made enquiries before deciding to propose. He told me he knew that I had an empty bank account and that I had no prospects whatsoever, but he did not hold this against me. He could offer me a future and could make me as happy and contented as his mother.

I was totally speechless. He considered this acquiescence, and thought my resistance was finally crumbling. He re-doubled his efforts.

He told me he knew my faults. He knew, for instance, that I can't cook. He was prepared to overlook this shortcoming. With his very own money he is going to send me to cookery classes, or better still he will send me to his mother for six months before the wedding, where I shall have the opportunity to learn about cooking and wifely duties.

'I don't wish to learn about cooking or housework,' I said irritably. 'When I get married – if I get married – I will have someone else to do all that. I will not lift a duster in anger. I refuse to do any housework. I have never done any, and I am not doing any now. Has not my ex-friend told you that I live in absolute squalor? My place is filled to overflowing with rubbish, the washing-up is piled in the sink for weeks on end. Housework is one of my pet hates. I hate it almost as much as I hate other people's mothers.'

He stared at me in disbelief. After some thought, he said that with so many negative qualities in the balance, he had no choice but to withdraw his offer. He was doing this reluctantly, he told me, as he rather liked the look of me, in spite of my size, my peculiar nose, my bow legs, my glasses, my limited intelligence and my superficial attitude to life.

With a sigh of relief I turned from him and started to walk home. He did the same. The distance grew between us. I glanced over my shoulder to see. He then stopped for a moment, and his outraged voice carried over the heads of startled late-night shoppers. 'And you are cross-eyed as well!'

Elaine W., 48, cashier

❧❧❧

I'd had my eye on the dark Mediterranean stranger as soon as he set foot in my place of work. I could hardly make out a word he said but this did not deter me from trying to chat him up.

At long last he asked me out for a meal. I donned my new Wonderbra under my tightest dress and I thought I looked gorgeous.

We set off on the bus to the local steakhouse. I ordered my steak well done and he asked for his rare. I thought this very exotic – ghastly, but exotic nonetheless.

We chatted amicably for a while. Well, he chatted and I smiled serenely. He could have said 'You look like an old goat' and I would have been none the wiser.

All of a sudden he leaned underneath the table, he'd obviously seen something. To my horror he picked up that oval-shaped piece of stuffing that had somehow worked its way out of my bra. 'What eez zis?' he asked, holding it up for the whole restaurant to see. I grabbed it quickly and shoved it into the bottom of my handbag. 'Ah, eet eez a ladies' thing, yes?' A lecherous grin spread across his face but I couldn't even begin to explain.

Luckily the meal came along. His steak was swimming in blood and, frankly, looked disgusting. 'Thees iz not cooked, you Eenglish cannot cook, except thee dumpling.' This remark he seemed to find side-splittingly funny. The couple at the next table watched speechlessly as he hacked into his steak, blood dripping down his chin.

111

He seemed to be able to put away vast amounts of red wine, but the only effect it had was to make him even more incoherent. I shuffled in my seat as his ramblings became more and more noisy and less and less intelligible.

He paid the bill and we left the restaurant, me crushed with embarrassment and him swaggering. While waiting for the bus he edged closer and closer. His hands were wandering nearer and nearer my lopsided boobs. All I could think of was his tongue being coated in a mixture of Bulls Blood and real blood, and was dreading the inevitable moment when he tried to stick his tongue down my throat.

In the distance I saw the blessed sight of my bus. Never before or since have I been so truly grateful to London Transport.

He turned me quickly in his arms and before I knew it his lips and mine were one, and the tongue sammo occurred. It was an extremely long kiss and as I tried to pull away, I heard and felt a snapping noise and a pulling sensation in my mouth. He had broken my brace plate – yes one of those yucky see-through jobs that you don't bother telling your friends about, after all why would they want to know?

My dentist was going to kill me.

I left him at the bus stop swaying from side to side mumbling that bloody annoying line, 'What eez zis, what eez zis, what eez zis?' Thankfully, the driver shut the doors before he could get on.

I told my dentist I'd broken my plate on a hard nut.

Lucy V., 30, mother of two young daughters

❧❧❧

Thirteen years ago, having just divorced my husband of thirty years, I was slowly becoming a recluse. A female friend of mine at the school where I was teaching at that time, wanting to play Cupid, arranged for a male member of her church to telephone me.

Having spoken for several weeks on the phone, we arranged to meet for the first time. When he asked where I wanted to go, not being a pub person I suggested he booked tickets to see the film *Caligula*, which was having its premiere somewhere in the city. I had recently seen *I Claudius* as a serial on the TV and assumed this to be a continuation film.

Next day in the staffroom I said that I was meeting Geoffrey and where we were going, and received knowing looks. I was touched that they were pleased that I was starting to face life again.

We met in a public car park and travelled in his car to the city, where we were soon sitting upstairs in a crowded cinema. The opening scene of the film had me slinking down in my seat, covered in confusion, getting redder and redder by the minute.

I'd invited a church-goer out for an evening of explicit pornography.

Jane E., 61, retired schoolteacher

❧❧❧

My most horrendous first date was probably the bloke's most horrendous first date ever as well. We met on Christmas Eve and, let's be honest, we were both drunk. The wine was flowing, I felt like the most glamorous woman alive and he started to chat me up. Things went well and by midnight he'd walked me home and we were kissing a very passionate goodbye.

I woke up the next day with my mum knocking on my bedroom door saying, 'Kevin's here to see you.' Slowly the memory of the previous night started to seep back into my brain. Then all of a sudden I remembered I'd asked him if he wanted to spend Christmas Day with me. My auntie normally has a party on the evening of Christmas Day, and this would be the first time in four years that I hadn't had a boyfriend to take with me.

I got dressed as quickly as possible and there he was, and he wasn't quite as good-looking as he'd seemed the night before. My dad was doing his best to keep a conversation going, but was quite obviously pleased to get out of the room when I appeared.

Kevin held out a package, all wrapped up with a little bow. As I was opening it he told me that he'd originally bought it for his ex-girlfriend for Christmas but he was giving it to me instead. I should have known at that point that it was a bad omen. I opened the package and there was this ugly – well, I thought so – gold chain staring up at me. I smiled weakly and put it on.

He then asked me if I fancied a walk. We ended up at his mother's house, and if ever there was a mother from hell she was it. She questioned me endlessly about myself – I expected her any moment to tell me to open wide so she could inspect my teeth. Finally she told me it was really good that Kevin had found a nice girlfriend. If we'd stayed much longer I think she'd have asked how I felt about chicken vol-au-vents for the wedding reception.

The worst part of the day was yet to come. In the evening we went to my auntie's house, a good ten miles away from my home, and I introduced him as a friend. He was obviously nervous, and who can blame him? In a house of strangers, the guest of an almost stranger. He tried to calm his nerves by having a shot of whisky – and another and another.

By half-past nine he was very drunk and quite clearly more confident. He proceeded to insult my grandma (fortunately she's deaf and didn't hear, but my mother did), tip a plate of food all over the floor, and shoot the contents of his whisky glass all over my aged Auntie Ethel and muck up the electrics in her wheelchair.

I couldn't stand his presence a second longer. I shoved him into the night, drunk and ten miles from home.

Oh, but I did give him his present back.

Eve G., 29, marketing co-ordinator

I'd had a bit of a crush on a particular man who often came to our local. So imagine my delight when he bought me a drink and went on to chat me up. We got on so well together, and when he asked me to go with him to watch Formula One motor racing the following Sunday, I was ecstatic.

I spent hours trying on different clothes to find the most suitable outfit. The day before, I had an expensive hairdo so I would look my best.

He said he would pick me up at eight a.m. I was up at six a.m. so I could be quite sure I'd be ready for him. I was so terribly excited that I sat looking through the window waiting for his car to pull up.

At last he arrived. I flew out of the house, jumped into his car and off we went. I chatted breathlessly to him, letting him know how thrilled I was to be going to such an event. I was so happy.

We were almost there when I suddenly looked down at my feet. My face froze in disbelief.

I had got my slippers on.

Not your nice little fluffy mule-type either. These were the slippers I'd had for ever. The sole was almost hanging off one of them. They were so old and worn it was almost impossible to determine their original style and colour. But they were still comfortable enough to slip on around the house and do the occasional bit of gardening in . . .

My date was not amused when I pointed out my dilemma. Not amused at all. He even suggested I stay in the car for the rest of the day.

However, I was determined to see the motor racing. So I spent the day walking with an exaggerated limp.

I felt that would account for my strange footwear.

As for my hero – he never did ask to see me with my shoes on.

Lorna I., 56, housewife

🐾🐾🐾

Nigel was tall, thin and my boss – and not to my personal taste. I fancied him about as much as I would a wet weekend in Bognor. But when he asked me out to see the newly released *Batman* I didn't hesitate to accept. After all, a cinema date, if not conducted in the back row, could hardly be a romantic minefield.

He turned up at my flat promptly, scaring off my sensitive flatmate with his moist handshake and leering stare. When we were alone, he announced that he had a surprise for me but first needed to use the loo. He was in there about ten minutes, during which I heard a lot of mysterious fumbling noises and started worrying about that, and the lateness of the hour. Finally, Nigel called from the bathroom for me to switch off all the lights and turn to face the window. After assuring me it would be a harmless surprise, I duly followed his instructions. When he told me to turn round, I saw . . .

BATMAN.

Nigel stood in the doorway, the only light coming from the street lamp outside. He raised his wings and there he was, fully kitted in a replica of Batman's suit,

117

complete with black rubber mask and pointy ears and knickers outside his tights.

He then called me Vicki – as in Vale – and swooped towards me. I was too busy laughing to receive the intended embrace. Instead I jumped out of the way and he almost fell out of the window. When he recovered his composure, he informed me we were going to the cinema in a hired 'Batmobile'. And no, he would not be changing out of his outfit.

With that, we motored towards the city centre, me with my eyes tightly shut, dying of embarrassment. He drove slowly in an open-topped old black Cadillac, adorned with a gigantic Bat motif, acknowledging the very excited pedestrians who surrounded us at every traffic light stop.

We parked ten minutes' walk from the cinema. I trailed as far behind Nigel as I could while he swooped along the pavement, stopping people and buses in their tracks.

When we took our seats in the cinema, practically the entire audience applauded him. I sank lower and lower into my seat. When the film started, he knew every damn line Batman spoke – and joined in with him, much to the annoyance of everyone within earshot. Apparently, Nigel had seen the film ten times, and it had only been out three weeks.

When we eventually got home, he kissed my cheek and his rubber mask stuck sweatily to my skin. I went to bed shellshocked, grateful at least that *The Shining* had not been his favourite film.

Laura W., 29, manager

❧❧❧

I met him at a dinner party. He seemed OK – a little bit older, a little bit wiser, a solid professional in the business community . . .

On the night, the doorbell rang, and I opened the door. Where was he? I looked down. 'Oh, there you are.' First bad point. He must have had heels on last Friday. Now, although I am 5ft 9in, I do like my men to be a little bit taller.

The vision became clearer. Below this wee, shiny, grinning face peering up at me was a green nylon tracksuit. I looked lower. Oh no. The black-and-white Adidas trainers loomed up. An outfit like this would have blended in well at any Wembley Cup Final. OK, so it was a casual date, but I would have expected jeans at the very least. I mean, will the bar down the road even let him in like that?

And so we drove off – past the bar we had intended going to. A wave of relief swept over me. He was obviously going back to his flat to change. And so I confidently asked where we were going. The reply was shocking – the unthinkable – we were going for a meal.

I now decided the probability of his gaining access to such a venue would be practically nil. I forgot that it was mid-week, and that any custom would be considered good custom. So among the suits, the dresses, and my jeans (thank goodness I'd worn my blazer), we were shown to our cosy table à deux. I grabbed the outside chair (to hasten my exit if necessary) and we ordered.

The food came and we started to eat. I never order spaghetti on a first date for obvious reasons. But he even had problems with a lettuce leaf. As he continued to talk through everything he ate, the leaf dangled from his mouth and down past his chin. I felt embarrassed for him and took over the talking role. I let my eyes wander, hoping he would be able to sort himself out – only to turn back my gaze to witness him ripping the lettuce leaf from his mouth with his bare hands, followed by an animal-like grunt.

It was around this point that I decided I really did want to be anywhere else but here with him.

Time went on, polite conversation passed our lips (and whatever else was dangling from his). At last, we got up to leave and I was pleased to see he insisted on paying the bill. But this is the part that left me lost for words. I myself sometimes carry my money in strange places – jean pockets, loose at the bottom of my handbag – but this initiative beats all the rest. He wellied £30 out of his right sock (which was on his foot at the time) and into the waitress's hand.

I felt for her. I even felt for myself by this stage.

I mean, was it a clean sock?

Was it a clean foot?

I really did not want to let my imagination loose on this line of thought. The fact that he kept his money down his sock was enough. Although since that evening, I have wondered if his American Express, driving licence, and whatever else can be found in men's wallets was down there too.

The waitress gave him his change and that was

returned to the sock. Hate to think what was happening to all that loose change.

We went back to 'our' car (as he was referring to his car by this time) and I asked if I could just go home as I was awfully tired. (Awfully tired of *him*, of course, but I'm too polite to say.)

The sight of my house was a welcome relief. But before I had managed to escape from 'our' car he had lunged towards me, lips a-puckered . . . there was no escape . . . I closed my eyes and prayed that no lettuce would pass my lips.

I scrambled out of 'our' car, muttered my goodbyes and ran for my front door – only to hear him tooting the horn enthusiastically – I turned my head – and this wee, shiny face was grinning back at me.

Next time . . . there wasn't one.

Rosie L., 26, public relations assistant

❧❧❧

I first met Rick in my local, where he was working behind the bar. He was dynamic, fun and incredibly sexy. We flirted like crazy, but I had 'another on my arm', so it was not to be. We lost touch when he moved away from the area.

Three months later I was unattached again, had moved into a place of my own, and often wondered what had happened to the object of my desire. One morning the phone rang – it was Rick! After talking for two hours, he asked me out the following Saturday.

I was wildly excited – I felt like a teenager again! My luck was about to change (for the worse, as it happened). I bought new clothes, new make-up, and two tickets for a jazz concert in town.

He was due to arrive at noon. By one o'clock I had worn holes in the carpet and tears streaked my new foundation. Suddenly the phone rang: 'Hi there! I'm in the Slug and Caterpillar. Come and join me for lunch.' The Slug and Caterpillar is the local 'dive' and wasn't quite what I had in mind on this romantic occasion, but what the hell. I touched up my mascara, threw forward my chest and put on my best smile.

Lunch was predominantly liquid. It was so wonderful to see him again and to be alone with him at last, that I was oblivious to the fact that he did most of the talking (about himself) and I failed to notice how glazed his beautiful blue eyes were becoming. I was in love!

Several beers later, my head was spinning and, 'ever the gentleman', he escorted me home so I could sleep off the alcohol before the concert that evening.

I woke up with a start at eight o'clock – the concert had started half an hour ago! I rushed to get ready, realizing that he had left. I ransacked my flat in search of my keys, only to find he had taken them himself and locked me in.

Since my doors are reinforced and I live on the second floor, I found myself breaking out of my own flat, clambering over a corrugated iron roof, shinning down a drainpipe and legging it to the concert.

I settled down as quietly as possible, looking nervously around for him to enter the concert hall – he hadn't taken his ticket. I needn't have worried.

A loud crash heralded his entrance and he slumped into a pew at the back. I pretended to be as disgusted as everyone else.

Halfway through the concert one of the main performers fainted. The second half was called off and the audience placated with a free glass of wine. Rick managed four or five.

I howled at him for ruining my day, but he looked so sorry we called a truce, laughed it off as a 'disastrous first date' and decided we would probably both feel better after something to eat.

The first thing Rick did in the restaurant was knock over a glass of wine at the bar, smashing it and splashing its spluttering owner. I dealt with this as best I could, apologizing profusely for his clumsiness.

When the meal arrived he sat swaying in his seat, much to the amusement of the other diners, before finally collapsing into his pizza. I patiently removed the mushrooms from his nostrils and guided him to the bathroom. Then I sheepishly returned to our table and finished my meal, trying to avoid the outraged stares.

Another furore caused me to look up, just in time to see a powerful-looking guy punch a bewildered Rick in the face and send him sprawling across the bar. This resulted in a tremendous scene with the frantic Italian owner. I hurriedly picked up the bill and we made an undignified exit.

I don't remember much about the walk home. But I awoke the next morning, disorientated and with an explosive head, on my own sofa. When I looked in the mirror, a mysteriously acquired shining black eye looked back.

I walked into the bedroom to find Rick snoring peacefully in my bed.

Emily Q., 29, teacher of information technology

6

'Devilish for us, too':
Men

When I heard a rumour about a local chap putting an ad in the personal column and getting bags of replies, I thought I'd have a shot. Twenty-six dates for £6.50 he got. Value for money, that, I would say.

Casual, easy-going, attractive pleasant gentleman seeks female to share whatever she fancies.

I thought 'casual' a better word than smart. 'Smart' was a bit starchy. And although the wording was a little loose, I did want to get replies. The 'attractive' might be pushing it a bit. I was no oil painting, but then I wasn't *un*attractive . . .

It cost me £11.50 plus VAT and I got two replies. I did nothing about them for a fortnight, so busy was I trying to convince myself that the readership of my local rag must be lower than that to which the other chap subscribed. When I did act, it seemed one had already been taken. So I met the second one.

Attractive. And silent. Laughed occasionally, but never spoke. Sipped her drink and gazed into space all evening. After three hours' talking to yourself it gets a bit tedious, so I decided she was just not interested. It seemed a reasonable assumption given the fact that she had not once met my eyes or initiated conversation. You can imagine how surprised I was when we pulled up outside her house and she loosened her seat belt, rolled over on to my knee – straddling my legs which were now trapped between her and the steering wheel – and glued her mouth to mine. I considered myself lucky to escape with my trousers.

Next I tried an introduction bureau. I spoke to them first before parting with any money, and gave them my details and my requirements. By now I had learned to be non-specific on the latter – it gave broader possibilities. But they said they'd soon have me 'suited'. So I met Angie.

Angie was full of goodness. Blonde and large and bubbling over with enthusiasm and a real lust for living. After a two-hour telephone conversation, which was interrupted sporadically by her hurling cheerful abuse at her children, I came off the phone with a higher bill, a new understanding of women's problems 'down under' and a slight feeling of nausea. Had I been a gynaecologist, it might have been a union made in heaven.

But I visited her once and she tried to feed me. I think it was going to be fried eggs. Pointlessly, she asked me how I like them. In retrospect I should have said 'On a clean plate'.

Drawing a still-greasy pan from once soapy water, she turned the gas up high and created spontaneous combustion by splattering two of the said items into a viciously spluttering rainbow-coloured scum.

But she meant well.

While she went next door to get sugar, I tried to tempt the dog with her generosity. But Rover, it seemed, knew this trick of old. After a quick sniff he coughed, sneezed and quick as you like vacated the premises.

A short time later, so did I.

Then there was the eighteen-stone factory packer. Described as a 'professional lady'. Later I learned why. Or at least I might have. She kept a nice home, in a nice area. Single, never married. The gods seemed to be smiling.

Giving little thought to my shock absorbers and suspension, I invited her out. I opened the car door for her. Size doesn't matter, I told myself. With difficulty she strapped herself in and looked me up and down as I did likewise. Lamb to the slaughter. I was the lamb.

'Are you a *big* man?' she asked me. Meaningfully.

I gulped, wondering if I had misheard. 'Are you?' she insisted. 'I only go out with *big* men.' She meant it.

I reassessed the 'size doesn't matter' theory and decided that even if I considered myself a 'big man' I'd certainly not be telling her.

Then came Mrs Save and Prosper. Late thirties, divorce pending who, when she was not comparing me to her not quite ex-husband, was trying to sell me insurance. When I sought some personal assurance she declared me 'adequate'.

Sigh.

Dating can be devilish for us men, too. But I keep trying.

Steve M., 41, journalist

❧❧❧

As I paced outside the appointed restaurant the Red Admirals in my stomach were fast becoming Sea Lords. Then I spotted a shady female figure across the darkened road, taking an occasional surveying shufti at me before embarking on the crossing.

'Lyn?' I enquired, pleasantly surprised, wondering why people never look the same as you imagine from how they sound on the phone. She wasn't beautiful, but she could be described at least as attractive. I decided that tonight was going to be great!

We chose a table in an alcove. In a way it was good that the Indian vegetarian restaurant was still completely empty, because it meant we could get to know each other in seclusion. Even at this point I knew she liked me from what my training had taught me. Her pupils were enlarged, and that only happens when a person is attracted to someone. Or sometimes it occurs when a person is extremely excited or maybe frightened, but that obviously wasn't the case here.

The owner was very attentive and I allowed my date to choose the gastronomic delights of our first evening together.

'Would you like some wine?' I asked, gazing into her enlarged pupils.

'I'm allergic to alcohol,' she declined coyly. She had a lovely shy smile.

She started to talk. I listened intently as her voice accelerated, gaining speed by the second. I could barely grasp anything as she spoke faster and faster, nearing even the speed of sound. My apprehension grew and I pondered whether my eardrums would burst if she ever reached Mach 1.

'Have you any brothers or sisters?' I innocently enquired.

'Keep it light,' she hissed, smiling.

The question mark on my face must have been obvious because she added, 'When we know each other better.'

The food arrived, adding excitement to our already electrified atmosphere. I swigged a calming amount of wine while she served us. The various dishes didn't appear too hot, but I was famished and, as politely as possible, began to shovel. Almost immediately my masticating jaws crawled to slow motion then stopped in mid-chew. It was cold! Everything she had ordered was stone, icy cold. And judging by her satisfied expression, it was supposed to be.

The Indian music wafted soothingly. She began to twitch. I asked her if she liked swimming.

'I'm allergic to the water,' she smiled, her pupils enlarging even more.

My palate had adjusted to the shock of freezing, spicy food and I continued eating.

'I'm just going to complain about the music,' she said quickly, disappearing. Moments later the strains of different Indian music came from the speakers.

She rejoined me, and this time she spoke even faster and her mouth was just a blur from the speed. I asked her about her parents.

'Keep it light,' she hissed again. She was smiling stiffly. Her eyes seemed as large as saucers, and the pupils had grown so big there were hardly any irises.

The establishment had begun to fill and it was the kind of place where even a whisper sounded loud. I leaned towards her, lowering my voice as much as possible. 'I'm very sorry, Lyn,' I apologized, sounding as empathetic as I could. 'I think you've been through a rough time . . .' – she twitched, the pupils seeming to fill her eyes – 'and it's been very nice meeting you, but I think it would be best if I got the bill.'

With that she grabbed her coat and dashed across the room. In tears, she screeched 'You must be mad!' and vanished into the night. I was left with several pairs of eyes dying to look at me but choosing to politely utilize the corner-of-the-eye technique.

'Could I have the bill please?' I croaked to the owner. He gave me a tepid smile, handing me the cost of my night of romance and passion.

'I think I've just upset the lady,' I offered lamely. 'I theenk zo,' came the disapproving reply, as I ventured through the gauntlet of steely eyes towards the exit.

I found myself praying that my blind date had caught a bus.

And was not lying in wait with a meat cleaver.

James N., 42, hypnotherapist

❧❧❧

I had kept on for ages to a work colleague of mine about how much I liked a woman I saw in the pub, and how I'd like to ask her out. Eventually I did. And she was fantastic company in every sense.

Imagine my surprise when I arrived to pick her up for dinner one night and my work colleague opened the door to me. He was my age and single, and I thought, 'Oh no, don't tell me she's seeing him too.'

Well, no, as I quickly discovered.

He was her son.

She had lied to me about her age, and I felt a complete fool. My friend from work asked me what I was doing there. I quickly made up an excuse about having a hospital appointment the next day and having forgotten to tell our boss, and could he do so for me.

He invited me in to have a drink, saying his mother was, as per usual, going out with some young stud shortly – adding 'More fool him. My mum'll give him a real ole runaround.'

I fled.

Dave V., 25, computer programmer

❧❧❧

Being employed as a credit control clerk was not the most thrilling of jobs – spending hours on end telephoning clients to beg them to part with my employer's money. It was only made bearable by imagining the no doubt beautiful faces behind the voices of the young women at the other end of the line.

Often I had been tempted to ask one of them out for a pre-Cilla blind date, but being only eighteen years old, my courage had not yet materialized and it was always left to the next time. However, fate was soon to take a helping hand.

During one of my calls beseeching cash, I left my

name and number, and asked the girl to call me back when the cheque was to be despatched. 'I used to know someone of that name,' said my client. 'Did you used to go to ***** Junior School?' She gave me her name and added, 'Surely you remember me? You once put two tennis balls in my school bag during assembly.'

Unfortunately, this wasn't much of a reminder as to this girl's identity. Living as I did backing on to private tennis courts, I was always well stocked with tennis balls. Any young female classmate who took my attention would receive an anonymous love gift of a couple of balls in her bag or desk.

Dashing, or what? (No, don't tell me.)

By now our telephone conversation had led to a meeting at a particular railway station at six p.m. the coming Saturday. To make sure we would recognize each other, we arranged to wear green tops. I would wear my new buttoned-down collared green shirt and she a green blouse.

Saturday could not come soon enough.

The station was a long way from my home, and I allowed two hours to drive there. Although I arrived in good time, I planned to wait until five minutes past six before walking into the station and swooning my date by the telephone kiosks.

Five minutes was taking too long! I just couldn't wait. I walked in at two minutes past.

My entry into the pages of Mills and Boon had arrived.

As I strode as confidently as I could towards the telephone kiosks, my heart missed a beat or two as I could not see anyone waiting there. Then I saw that there was another block of phone kiosks on the other side of the concourse. Standing in front of that block was a girl in a green blouse.

This fairy story had now taken a decidedly downward turn. Somewhere the script had gone askew, because what must surely have been a beautiful duckling to warrant two tennis balls had grown into a swan who was definitely not my type.

My mind now started racing as I thought of how I could make an exit. Perhaps she wouldn't know it was me. I looked at my watch, giving the impression – so I hoped – that I could not see the person I was supposed to meet and that I would soon be on my way.

After a few minutes of this uncomfortable fidgeting, some friends of the girl arrived to catch a train. As they started talking, nods and gestures were directed at me, but I made out that I didn't notice.

Finally, one of these friends walked over and asked, 'Are you meeting a girl named June?' Despite my heart screaming out 'No', I found my mouth saying 'Yes'. I walked over to the kiosks, smiling nervously, still half-considering a dramatic bolt for the exit.

My date mentioned going for a drink, but I managed to persuade her to go to the cinema. It would be dark in there. I tried to be as pleasant as I could manage, but the evening could not pass quickly enough.

Afterwards, only one awkward question remained. How could I ask for the return of my balls?

Larry B., 43, accounts manager

❦❦❦

Wandering around the dreary wet streets one September afternoon, I happened upon an interesting-looking clothes shop. As much out of a need for warmth as for clothing I ventured in. The accent hit me a millisecond before the waft of Samsara. She was beautiful and very French. I was lost.

After a conversation with Chantal, I left the store and continued my meandering. But she played on my mind, and by four p.m. I had walked a dozen times past the shop, trying to pluck up the courage to give her the flowers clutched wilting in my hands. I finally walked in and persuaded her to go out with me the following Thursday for dinner.

I picked her up, a vision in black short skirt and fitted top, and drove to my favourite 'can't fail' venue. I don't smoke, and when she asked me if she could, I told her this and said that most of my friends wait until they are out of the car. She proceeded to light up a Gauloise and chain-smoked for the remainder of the journey.

We arrived and took our places, listening to the live music and sipping our first glass of red wine. The menus arrived, but she told me that she had already eaten and only wanted to drink. I was surprised, for it was to have been a dinner date, but, still unfazed, I ordered my main course and resolved to spend the saved dinner money on another bottle of wine for her.

With the second glass, she informed me that she was not very good at holding her alcohol. She then proved the point by knocking the remainder of the wine over the white tablecloth and my trousers, fortunately also dark in colour. I rushed to the men's room, brushing aside her apologies in my hurry to avoid the barely hidden smiles of the diners sitting nearby.

On my return there was another almost full bottle of wine sitting on the table; and an empty plate lay in front of my chair. My food had arrived.

'It was getting cold,' she explained, 'so I ate it.'

After the rest of the wine and remaining cigarettes for her, and another glass of water for me, I paid the bill and we left.

Swayed by her now fluid figure leaning against me, I put doubt out of my mind and went to show her off at a friend's party. The night was still young and hope sprung eternal.

Introductions over, I left her chatting to the assembled small crowd of guests in the sitting-room while I went to the kitchen. I wanted to crow to those men still on their own or with lesser companions for the night, and also to my best friend Luke, the host.

Suitably impressed though he was, his wife wasn't. She came through a third time to search for more crisps and nuts. The French woman, we were informed, must have worms. As fast as Heather filled the bowls up, Chantal emptied them, mentioning all the time that she wasn't really hungry.

Arriving late as we had because of 'dinner' earlier, we had missed the food. So too had Luke, who had also just arrived after picking up his parents from the station. Looking around for his dinner, he asked his wife where it was. 'In the microwave,' was the reply.

I sensed before I knew for certain that the empty plate revolving there in the shielded light had been visited earlier. Yes, Chantal confirmed, she'd eaten its contents when everyone had been in the garden.

Luke actually found it quite funny, but I found it time to go. Nothing was worth this and Chantal was getting drunker, and more obvious with the men, and more hated by the women, every passing moment.

After another dozen Gauloises we arrived back at her shared flat. She stood up and was sick into the passenger well of my car before sitting down with a grunt on the pavement. I heaved her to her feet. She just about managed to tell me that I couldn't come in as her boyfriend (boyfriend? what boyfriend?) would be asleep.

I parked her against the front door before ringing the bell and leaping back into my reeking car. I drove away as fast as I could, windows and sun roof wide open.

Romance and shopping – you can keep 'em.

Mark Y., 34, advertising manager

🐞🐞🐞

I was about fifteen, at one of those teenage parties where everyone sits around on the floor necking. I got chatting to a blonde girl my age, quite plump but very pretty.

We ended up sitting under a table, sharing half a bottle of VP sherry and getting totally pissed.

At last, emboldened by booze, I lunged at her for a snog. As my tongue slithered into her mouth, I found . . .

Apart from the four at the front, she'd got no teeth.
Ken T., 42, journalist

❦❦❦

It was my one and only blind date.

It started when I went on holiday with three friends, camping in the countryside. We met four girls who were staying on the same campsite and we paired off. At the end of the week our cases were packed and we said goodbye. However, my best friend Sam continued to see the girl he'd met for several weeks after the holiday.

One night in the pub, Sam told me that his girlfriend had been showing the holiday photographs to her friends at work. One of them fancied me, and wanted a date. Being in between girls at that time and the only lad in my group without a steady girlfriend I agreed to a blind date. Arrangements were made for me to go with Sam on a double date.

From this point on things started to go downhill. Sam and I set out in his aging wreck of a car. One door was completely jammed, the other could only be opened from the outside. Once in the car, Sam had to climb out of his window to let me out. I thought, this will really impress my new date.

The car managed to get us to the rendezvous on time. After several nervous moments' wait the two girls appeared. My expectations sank out of sight. She was so thin she must have been wearing braces to hold up her skirt and her face was covered in spots. I'm no oil painting, but I wanted to run away. I was stuck there, no transport home and in a town I didn't know. Not wanting to hurt the girl's feelings, I grinned and made polite small talk as we made our way to a local pub.

The girls sat down and Sam and I went to get the drinks. The air turned blue with the threats and insults I threw at him for setting me up with an Olive Oyl lookalike.

We joined the two girls at a seat near to an open window. It was one of those sort of pubs where you don't look twice at anybody. The windows were fitted with wire mesh to save them from missiles. As we chatted away, young boys were jumping up at the outside of the open window and spitting through it. The two girls didn't bat an eyelid and carried on as though nothing was amiss.

I suggested we move to a pub with a little less wildlife.

After a few minutes' drive we pulled into what I thought was a derelict street. All the houses were boarded up or falling down. Sam stopped the car outside a detached building. All the windows and doors that we could see were covered by large wooden boards.

Sam climbed out of his window and let the rest of us out. The girls walked to the side of the building where there was a heavy steel door. It swung open and we entered a dark smoke-filled bar room. It was also filled with very heavy-duty looking guys. It was as though the music stopped and everybody stared at me and Sam.

I had never been so scared in my life.

Suddenly someone recognized the girls and

everything was all right. Sort of. Sam looked at me and said 'Just the one drink?'

'Make it a half,' I said.

After we had quickly downed our drinks I made an excuse for me and Sam to go home early. So off we went to the house where Sam's girlfriend lived. He went in to say goodbye while I stayed in the car with my blind date. She couldn't take a hint – or I didn't make it clear – but she was coming on strong and I couldn't back away any further.

Just then a news flash came on the radio: Jimi Hendrix was dead. Although I liked some of his music I couldn't be classed as an ardent fan. But I pretended to be gutted. Too devastated to think about kissing and cuddling. It was all I could do to stop the tears from flowing down my cheeks.

Eventually Sam came out of the house and I was saved from my torment. I never went on a blind date again, not ever.

Tony K., 42, police officer

🐾🐾🐾

The year was 1987. I was nineteen years old, and had just started work after my A-levels. I had never been tremendously successful with the opposite sex up to that time, so you can imagine my excitement on being approached by a reasonably attractive girl and asked for a date!

I gladly accepted this offer, and insisted that I take

her out for a meal, all expenses paid. We arranged the time and day, and she left me to choose the location.

My intention from that moment on was to sweep her off her feet. So off I went to Burtons to purchase my first-ever suit. Now what about a location? Not being very experienced at this sort of thing, I asked my boss to recommend a suitable venue. He eagerly wrote down the address of a very good restaurant he knew in the next town (I didn't find out till later that he practically had shares in the said establishment).

My car at the time was a Mark IV Ford Cortina, nice car but it only had a radio. To ensure a pleasant ambience after the meal I would need a tape player. I wanted to guarantee those sweet romantic melodies that would – I hoped – aid my progress in the canoodling stakes!

The only cassette player I could afford came with wires that wouldn't quite reach the speakers at either side of the car's back shelf. So to save time (this was the afternoon of the date), I struggled to place both speakers in one corner of the car and stretch the wires across and up the back seat to them.

My 'passion wagon' now prepared, I rushed off to shower for the fourth time that day (well, you want to be clean, don't you?) before donning my new suit and dousing myself in aftershave. Finally ready, I set off to pick up my date.

After arriving at her parents' house and opening the car door for her (for effect), she politely informed me that she had invited a friend along and would I pick her up too! So much for a candlelit dinner for two, I thought. But what could I do? This 'friend' was someone I knew from church – I could hardly turn her down . . .

We arrived at the friend's house. As I showed her into the back seat, she chose to sit down right on top of the speaker wires that had taken me so long to install, snapping them both! At this, Whitney Houston stopped singing abruptly, and that was the end of the *Greatest Love* album as far as that night was concerned.

The restaurant was a lovely place. Too lovely, in fact, since loveliness generally equates to expense and I had only £50 left in my wallet and now another mouth to feed. Fortunately, on realizing this, my appetite began to diminish. I had to do a little persuasion regarding food recommendations ('everyone skips main courses these days' type of thing) and pretend I had just started a new wonder-diet. So by the end of the meal I had managed to keep the final bill down to £47.50 – the other £2.50 I left as a tip!

Meal over, I was anxious to ditch our chaperon and head for a quiet country lane. On the way back to her house, things really began to go wrong. My car-owning friends and I had recently had some trouble (car doors kicked in and windows smashed) with a gang of thugs who also drove around our little town in convoy. I was now aware that a suspicious white van had been following us for quite some time. Worse still, the driver had started flashing me and beeping his horn as I attempted to lose him all around the town.

After a hectic chase, traffic lights eventually stopped our storming progress. Sure enough, my pursuer got out of the van. A well-built fellow, I noticed – very well-built – as he approached my car swearing violently.

Brave to the last I got out to face him, and tensed myself to receive the first blow.

But instead of punching me unconscious, he presented me with a Cortina wheel-trim that he had seen fall off my car back at the restaurant and had been trying to give me back ever since. After a few more four-letter words he departed peaceably. I paused for a moment to allow the colour to re-enter my face, dumped the wheel-trim in the boot and sped off.

Despite the car chase, my date was still fairly happy with the idea of an evening drive in the countryside. So, after dropping off the gooseberry, we headed for the hills. At ten p.m. we finally reached the most out of the way country track I could find, and parked facing a five-bar gate for a bit of a snoggette.

My date turned out to be a far more overwhelming and passionate kisser than I had expected, so at eleven p.m. I was relieved to be informed that we had better head home as she had an early start in the morning.

I quickly started the car, and since there was no room to turn round, I began to reverse back along the dark country track. There was no moon that night, so I had to rely on the Cortina's pale reversing lights to guide me – through a badly steamed-up rear window.

Suddenly we felt a jolt and heard a crash as the front of the car lurched upwards and came to rest with the bonnet pointing more than a little bit skyward. Yes, you guessed it, I had reversed into a ditch.

Fortunately only one back wheel on the passenger side had slipped in – maybe I could push the car out, I thought. Tears began to well up in my date's eyes as I climbed into the ditch ready to push. I felt the clammy

wetness of mud fill my shoes and surround my ankles.
After two minutes I knew that there was no way I could
move that car.

Perhaps if we both tried . . .

On hearing this suggestion my date promptly locked
herself in and began weeping openly.

Eventually she agreed to try to drive the car forwards
while I pushed. Unfortunately, however, as her foot
hit the accelerator the back wheels simply spun on the
spot, coating me and my new suit in a thick layer of
mud.

Now resembling a creature from the black lagoon, I
set off in the pitch darkness to look for help. At
midnight, after tripping and stumbling across what
seemed like a mile of rough terrain, I spotted a light in
the distance. A house – I was saved!

The home-owner opened his door just wide enough
to see my mud-stained frame. For some reason he
appeared at first rather reluctant to help me . . . But
after five minutes of begging, he agreed to call for the
AA.

It was two a.m. before I finally found the car again.
My date had stopped weeping.

She was now bawling her eyes out.

I thought better of putting my muddy arm round
her to comfort her.

At three a.m. I noticed yellow lights in the distance
and ran towards our saviour. It has to be said that the
AA patrol did extremely well not to laugh as I showed
him our predicament.

Once towed out of the ditch, the car seemed to drive
well enough and off we went home at three-thirty.

Funnily enough, the relationship did not last very long after this incident. She ran off with a hotel manager from down south, and I went on to find another woman to whom I am now married and hope to live happily ever after . . .

Paul I., 25, deputy computer manager

❧❧❧

I was to start a new job in the January, and the company asked me if I'd like to go to the office Christmas party first to meet the rest of the staff.

My eyes locked on to a stunning woman: blonde punk hair, black eyes, tight black dress and calf-high boots. I went over and started chatting to her. I was desperate to impress, clutching a glass of unspeakably awful white wine and nervously knocking back mouthfuls of peanuts.

Suddenly, in mid-guffaw, a peanut shot out of my mouth. It soared about five yards up in the air, curving in a perfect trajectory. Travelling well, it landed in her boot.

She very nobly pretended not to notice. I retreated in utter humiliation. I saw her later, hobbling to the ladies to shake it out.

It took me about six months to stop going red and to ask her for a date.

But life is crammed with vital lessons. I've now informed our son of the total incompatibility of any species of nut and chatting up women.

Ken T., 42, journalist

❦❦❦

About six or seven years ago, I was sitting in a big-city pub when a woman came in and ordered a drink.

My attraction to her was instant. She was small and slender, and had a stud through one side of her nose, lots of rings on her fingers and a tattoo. Despite that, I found her very attractive. Those sorts of thing are just the fashion, I thought. I'm sure she has a really sweet, caring nature. But before I could get the chance to start any sort of conversation with her, she finished her drink and left.

I never saw her again until about a month ago. But her effect on me was just as strong as the first time I'd seen her. As I stared at her, I knocked over my drink. She smiled at this, and we began talking. We had a few drinks, but all too soon it was time for me to go for my train. However, much to my delight, she asked me to meet her again. She gave me her telephone number with instructions to call her any time I wanted.

I was ecstatic. I just knew she was going to be everything I wanted: sexy, loving, funny, vulnerable.

We met a couple of days later, and went to a Chinese restaurant for dinner. Over the sweet and sour, I told her of my feelings for her and the effect she had on me. She was somewhat surprised, but said that she fancied me when she saw me in the pub.

Frequently, during the meal, she reached over the table to hold my hand. I could not believe my good fortune.

I was in love.

Towards the end of the meal, and three-quarters down the bottle of Asti Spumante (most of which she had drunk), she let it slip that she'd been out of circulation for a few years.

'Oh,' I said, 'been working abroad?'

'No,' she said, 'armed robbery.'

Gary S., 28, clerical officer

7
'So this is new?':
Men and Women in the 1930s-1950s

1930s

I met this girl – smart young woman she was – in a pub one night. I was about eighteen at the time. We got chatting, and I asked her if she wanted to go to a 'posh' dinner dance the next night. She agreed, so I said I'd pick her up at seven-thirty and drive along to this dance, at a hall some fifteen miles away.

Well, it was a cloudy evening with rain threatening. I arrived at her place on time, and she was all ready. She was looking very lovely with her best frock on, with lots of fluffy underskirts (that was the fashion then). She had lovely legs which looked gorgeous in shimmering silky nylon stockings. She'd had her hair done up nice, too.

When I took her outside to my motorbike, her face dropped. Apparently, she'd been expecting at least a decent car for transport!

Nevertheless, I persuaded her that it would be all right on the pillion, and that we'd be there quick. So she tied a headscarf on (we didn't wear helmets in those days, but I used to wear my flat cap back to front when

I rode my motorbike). Off we set.

And it started to rain. More groans and moans from the back. Her make-up was running, she yelled, and her legs were stinging.

'Hang on, luv,' I shouted. 'We'll soon be there.' I went faster.

We parked the bike and went up the steps of the hall. Hundreds of people were arriving, all 'poshed up' for the 'do'. At this point, my date was absolutely seething. I must admit, her windswept permed hair and streaky face make-up looked pretty wild. She didn't blend in very well with all the other smooth and sophisticated guests.

But the final crunch came when one of her stockings collapsed and fell round her ankle in a crinkled heap. Some acid from the battery on my motorbike had splashed on to her legs.

She fumed, complained and sulked all night. It was awful.

We never dated again.

I did buy her some new stockings a week later, but she told me to tie them round my neck and hang myself.

Albert J., 75, retired builder

🐾🐾🐾

1940s

MEN

It was a Sunday, 1944.

I was home on leave from the services, and had just met a nice girl. She asked me home to her house to meet her mum.

Her mum said, 'You may as well stay for tea, now you're here.' I sat down to a plate of salad, tomatoes, etc.

Halfway through the meal, I saw on my lettuce a big green caterpillar. Rather than embarrass her mum, I folded it up in a leaf of lettuce and ate it.

My girlfriend saw me do it, but did not say a word till we got outside. Then she said, 'I think you're the bravest man I've ever met.'

I never saw her from that day to this.

So you think hellish dates are new?

Bill S., 73, retired bookkeeper

🐛🐛🐛

At seventeen, Mike was on the look-out for a girlfriend, but daren't make any approaches even though most of the local lasses fancied him.

He'd a problem: shyness. He'd blush the deepest crimson if a girl so much as fluttered an eyelash at him. They knew his weakness and teased him.

An apprentice bricklayer, he was subject to ribaldry from workmen and the other apprentices, Harry the joiner's mate and me, who was learning plumbing.

Harry tried to help overcome Mike's apprehensions by chatting up the girls for him. He'd even fix foursome dates, but they weren't a success. Mike would become

149

a stuttering, red-faced idiot, sticking closer to Harry than to his date. We'd get him to a dance, and he'd leave in a hurry.

Harry grumbled, 'Waste o' time trying t' get him organized. He runs before they've time to give him the come hither.' For his part, Mike would invent romantic attachments, and grew angry when we laughed at him.

Then came a day when he proudly announced he'd a date with Janey Gibson. This was the ultimate. Janey was the most desirable and elusive lass in the area, a peach, pick of the bunch. Janey Gibson and Mike Coombes?

Impossible.

Neither Harry nor I had had any success with her. So what chance had he?

We couldn't accept it and decided it was another of his fantasies. Yet he persisted, and eventually it seemed she might have agreed to meet him.

But we had reservations. 'Aw, she's havin' you on,' claimed Harry. 'She'll not turn up.' I chipped in with an invidious 'She'll be doing it for a bet.'

Mike was adamant she'd promised to take a stroll with him if it was a fine evening. 'I'll take her up Trilling, past the golf course,' he boasted. Anxious to prove he wasn't lying, he went on: 'Look, I'm meeting her at the top of Trilling Lane at seven. You can check if you want, but keep out the way, don't spoil things for me.'

So he convinced us. Harry told him, 'We wouldn't dream of spoiling your date, pal. I wish you luck.'

Mike gloated. 'Yeah, you've both tried to take her out and she didn't want to know, did she?'

150

We kept clear of Trilling Lane, and quizzed him the following morning. At first he was loath to spill the beans, but persistence wore him down.

Harry and I, in unison: 'How d'you get on last night?'

Harry: 'No problems? Did she turn up?'

Mike, indignant: ''Course she turned up.'

Me: 'Got on all right then? When you seeing her again?'

He pursed his lips: 'Hummm . . . it's doubtful, extremely doubtful.'

Harry and I chorused: 'Oh!'

Probably considering Mike might have attempted the over-amorous, Harry suggested he could have 'overstepped the mark.'

Mike shook his head. 'Nowt like that. I'm too shy and you know it.'

We eventually got the story. He paused to word his explanation carefully. We waited, then he went on.

'I'm not the only one who's shy. Janey's as bad as me; worse. We walked half a mile without a word. Then I managed to say, "It's a nice evening." She nodded.

'After another quarter mile, I said, "I like the way you have your hair done." She smiled and nodded.

'At the top of Meadow Lane I was tongue-tied, seeking something to talk about. Then I saw a horse in the next field; it had been rolling in mud. I just blurted out, "Look at that great, big, dirty, filthy horse."

'Even as I spoke we reached a gap in the hedge where Janey got a real vision of Dobbin. He had an enormous . . . Obviously a stallion having beautiful thoughts.'

Harry and I got the picture; we laughed like drains

before I managed to say, 'Go on, what happened next?'

He grunted. 'I didn't blush – I laughed and couldn't stop. Janey did the blushing; worse than you've ever seen me. She muttered through tight lips, "I'm going back," and she shot off. I never caught up with her.'

He began to laugh, a titter at first, but it grew. Soon everyone on the building site could hear him. He wiped his tears and said, 'Yeah, it's doubtful she'll go out with me agen an' I didn't do owt. Except laugh . . .'

I don't remember ever seeing him blush again.

Ned D., 72, retired owner of small business

❦❦❦

When I was stationed abroad, most of the unattached army lads had pen friends.

One of my closest chums came off a middle class well-to-do family. He showed me a snap of a stunning eighteen-year-old girl and said she was his cousin, at present working in a London hospital.

After her first two letters it got all so romantic.

She told me, 'I enjoy getting your letters so much. I like to hear all about what you are doing.' She made her letters lively and amusing, and told me catty stories about the other young nurses and their officer patients.

I was not due back in England for another year. I spent the time imagining meeting her for the first time on Victoria station.

When it finally happened . . .

She was about 5ft 10 in; I'm only 5 ft 3 in.

The long and short of it was that she was not the petite vision of loveliness I'd imagined, and her past little anecdotes didn't seem quite so funny any more. She was a big-busted woman, and towered over me more like a bodyguard than a lover. She wore a 'Sam Brown' and gave me a military salute.

Instead of being caught up in some giddy whirl of romance, we ended up in Lyons Corner House with me spilling the tea.

Then I went to the nearest pub and spilled a hell of a lot of beer.

Arthur G., 67, retired

༖༖༖

WOMEN

My date, both hilarious and embarrassing, happened during the last war. My closest friend had met a Canadian soldier one evening. On the second date it was suggested that he bring a pal along, and she would obligingly take me.

Because it was wartime and the blackout, we met inside a tube station. Here I got my first glimpse of my 'blind date'. After the introductions, and to break the ice, we made our way to a public house. I was not impressed, and by the look on his face, neither was he.

Excusing ourselves to go to the Ladies (girls always go in twos, I don't know why), my friend enquired of me: 'Do you like yours?' 'No, he's wearing big boots. Do

153

you like yours?' 'I don't like his moustache,' said my friend.

In between loud giggles and applying more lipstick we decided to use another exit, and leave the two soldiers in the bar.

Outside, still laughing heartily at what we had done, we made our way through a sand-bagged entrance into the next pub.

There at the bar were the two soldiers, ordering pints.

May N., 70, retired teacher

🐞🐞🐞

Nothing could have dampened my ardour – not food rationing nor any of the shortages that immediately followed the end of the war.

He was a successful grocer, I a newly fledged secretary ready to embrace the romantic notions so faithfully promised by the women's magazines and my diet of sloppy films and novels.

My parents were a bit sniffy about him being 'in trade', but were grudgingly impressed when he swept me off in his limousine for a candle-lit dinner. Then, as the months went by, there were the flowers and other tender tributes of affection.

I thought my prince had come. Something was surely about to happen.

'I've got something very special for you tonight,' he breathed tenderly.

Could this be the ring at last? I wondered.

'Please don't open it until you are in the house.'

I left the car and blew him a kiss as I closed the front door. Clutching my package I gently opened it and let out a scream.

My mother rushed from her bedroom. 'Look what he's given me,' I gasped. Turning back the paper we both stared down at half a pound of boiled ham. 'How could he, how could he do this to me?'

'What a man,' said Mother, the keeper of the ration books. 'How wonderful, we haven't seen ham for ages. You see it's thirty-two points a pound.'

'That's it,' I wept. 'It's over. I thought he was my prince, but he's gammoned me.'

Margaret B., 66, retired public relations consultant

🐞🐞🐞

1950s

MEN

I was a young soldier stationed abroad, where life was hectic and the drink cheap; though sadly there were not enough unattached English women to go round, so competition was fierce!

One evening at a party I met a very attractive nurse who was serving at the nearby hospital. She agreed to go out with me on the following Saturday, when she came off duty. Much to my delight, for I thought my luck was changing.

On the agreed day I was as ready and as keen as possible, for I had high hopes of the evening.

All went well till I arrived at the nurses' quarters, where I was told she had been delayed on duty. But she had sent a message that I should be given tea in the nurses' sitting-room while I waited. There was only one other person having tea that afternoon, for most of the nurses had dashed off to their dates or whatever for the Saturday night.

That other person was the matron, an imposing figure clad largely in a pure white heavily starched apron. She also possessed a very loud upper-class voice; being a very young soldier at the time I was delighted to let her dominate the conversation.

However, it was not long before I noticed her bosom. On one side was the traditional reversed watch; on the other, two medals dangling from their ribbons and swaying gently as she spoke. The terrible thing was that I found myself being mesmerized by the swaying medals. However hard I tried I was unable to take my eyes off them, and wherever I looked my eyes were drawn back to those swaying medals . . .

Young as I was, I knew that it was not very good manners to stare at one's host's left bosom, however heavily starched and bemedalled it might be. I could feel myself going red and spluttering, for I was unable to drag my eyes away while fighting hard to maintain my part in the conversation. I was not helped by having – in true British fashion – a cup of tea and a plate with a sandwich in my hands, which were soon shaking, partly with nervous laughter and partly in sheer terror of this woman. Knowing what a sorry figure I was making only made it worse, and my role in the conversation was soon reduced to grunts and nods as I tried not to giggle with nerves.

But the last straw came when this fearsome matron indulged in some shop talk. 'Ah you're with the XX Regiment, cut the b---s off one of your soldiers this morning.'

At which point I lost all control and dropped the cup, saucer, plate and sandwich, still staring at her left bosom and those terrible medals while the tea soaked into my lap. I was so dripping with tea and crumbs, I hardly noticed my date for the evening coming into the room. But I heard the matron's booming cut-glass voice, 'This is one of yours.' In a tone that suggested 'This' was something nasty on a shoe.

I'll not pretend the date was a success. I'd lost my nerve and my powers of conversation, not helped by the unfortunately placed, dark wet tea marks on my best light-coloured trousers. The poor woman must have wondered at her sanity in agreeing to meet me for such a wasted Saturday night. I'll admit too that I've never dated a nurse since that day, for whenever tempted, the image of that matron has arisen, and the day when from being a dashing (well, relatively) young soldier I was reduced to 'This', a speechless youth with a wet lap.

Bob C., 58, city guide

Just where the evening started to go wrong is difficult now to recollect. Sheila and I had spent two very nice evenings together since our meeting three weeks earlier. She was a staff nurse at the local hospital, and I was on leave from Africa and teetotal while recovering from a tropical fever. Life was good, and this evening I had booked tickets for a charity ball.

The seven-thirty bus arrived, and all the passengers alighted. No Sheila. I turned away. 'Excuse me, are you William?' I turned back to see who was speaking. 'I'm Pam.' She stood there, wearing a belted white raincoat over a red dress, with an attractive smile.

'I have a message from Sheila, she can't make it tonight and she is so sorry. Something came up.' I offered Pam the ball tickets, but she said they would be no use to her as she was going to the Palais on her own. Instead, she agreed to come with me, as she was dressed for dancing.

Making conversation was easy, and after collecting the car we drove to the ball. En route we passed a country pub and I suggested stopping for a drink. Her reaction was 'That's a bar, they serve alcohol' so fiercely that I drove on.

At the ball she danced well and we enjoyed each other's company. I suggested a drink and steered us both to the bar. 'What will you have?' I asked.

'Is it all alcoholic?' A few minutes for thought. 'A brandy and port, please.' By now I was quite confused, and asked 'Are you sure?' 'Yes,' she said.

Then we danced again for a while, chatting normally, and I relaxed. Then she excused herself to speak to a friend of hers and suggested that I could ask someone else to dance. It made a change, and when I looked across she was chatting to a number of women. During a 'ladies' excuse me' she came back. This time, she didn't have so much to say.

Then the highlight of the evening was announced – a spot waltz – and we took the floor. The spot stopped and the light was just about on us. The master of ceremonies came up as the music stopped and presented me with a gold cigarette-lighter and Pam a large bottle of Chanel perfume. Very handsome gifts. After the applause had died down the music started up and we made a circuit of the dance floor, slowly.

When we arrived back at the presentation spot, the MC stepped out and asked us to stop for a moment. He said that he was sorry, but there'd been a mistake. The prizes should have gone to a couple behind us and at the place where the spotlight struck the floor.

I was just handing back the lighter when my companion shouted 'Not bloody likely' and aimed a punch at the MC. She missed and dropped the perfume bottle as she fell. I caught the bottle but missed her. She climbed to her feet, enraged, and tried to grab the bottle. The organizers came and, with her shouting and swearing, we were bundled out of the hall.

Pam, to my horror and absolute surprise, was away with the composers Brahms and Liszt.

I got her to the car and stopped some distance away to ask where she lived. To add to my anguish, a police patrol car pulled in in front of us. Oh, no. What now?

The police told me my back light was faulty. Somebody had backed into the car while we were at the ball, and broken one of the lights. They advised me to get it fixed. Suddenly there came the sound of a slurred voice. 'What do those nosy bloody coppers want?' They told her, 'Lucky you are not driving, madam.' To a background of abusive remarks I managed to persuade them that I had not been drinking. They advised me to get her home to bed.

Eventually she gave me her address. I found the house easily enough, but she could not find the key. So I rang the doorbell and propped her against the door jamb. A pyjama-clad gentleman whipped open the door, yelling 'How dare you bring her home in this state?'

He aimed a punch at me. I dodged, thrust Pam into his arms and fled.

William D., 62, college welfare officer

🌺🌺🌺

When I was twenty-five years old, I served as doorman at the Town Hall Saturday night dances. Most of the dancers were teenagers, but one night I saw a young woman of about twenty-three or twenty-four. As I did not see anyone with her, I asked her to dance, and then to go for a drink. During the conversation she agreed to go to the cinema with me the following evening.

At the cinema we settled into a double seat on the back row with all the other couples. Three-quarters of the way through the film she suggested we go for a walk. As it had been raining when we went into the cinema, I thought 'Ay ay!'

We set off for a local quarry. The road to the quarry had pine trees along both sides, and to get out of the rain we went into the trees. She arranged her umbrella so we could stand dry beneath. My heart began to beat faster, I started to reach out to her . . . And she took out a harmonica from her pocket and began to play.

She told me she used to play duets in the bathroom, with her aged father on the trombone.

'Blow this!' I thought. 'Let me get her home!' And it continued to pour down with rain.

On reaching the entrance to the estate where she lived she suggested that we go into the trees just off the main path for a goodnight kiss. We were just having a second kiss when she went limp in my arms. As I managed to catch her before she fell in the muddy path I thought, Hell! I'm not that good a kisser!

I thought she must be ill. When she came to I asked if she felt unwell, and she replied, 'I just wanted to see what you would do.' I told her: 'You scared the life out of me. Don't do that again, as I won't catch you next time.'

We resumed kissing and she passed out again!

I did not catch her this time, and she landed in the mud with the rain beating on her face. I thought, if anyone comes by now they will phone the police. I was in such a panic I could not even think of her name. She came round after two or three minutes but it seemed like hours.

I then had to take her home and try to explain to her father what had happened. It turned out she had been courting a boy for three years, when he up and married someone else. She had a nervous breakdown, and I was the first chap she had gone out with since. And, sorry as I felt for her, for the last time I fear. If it had been a saxophone, now ...

Derek E., 63, shop manager

🐾🐾🐾

I remember once taking a young woman out to the cinema on a date (or rather, trying to take her out to the cinema – because I never actually got her there).

I'd arranged to pick her up from her home where she lived with her family, she being about seventeen and I eighteen. The year would be about 1958-59.

I arrived early and knocked at the door. Her mother – a huge, dominant woman – let me in. 'Do come in and sit down,' she said, 'we're just about to have our tea – so you can join us. I've set a place for you.'

She gave me no chance to decline, and I was duly sat down at the table opposite to Rosanne – my 'date'. From then on in it was all Ros's mum – her irritating neighbours, the shocking price of Hovis – even Ros couldn't get a word in edgeways.

The meal was fried fish (I can see it glistening now), chips and peas. Unfortunately, I didn't eat fish. I told Ros's mum. It was already loaded up on my plate, however, and – according to Ros's mum – 'It would do me good' and I was to 'get it down' me. I wasn't even hungry anyway. I'd already had my tea at home. But the pressure on me to eat was incredible. I could tell that Ros was so embarrassed by this – even though she was probably used to it all.

I simply could not bring myself to eat that fish. I kept delaying the awful, inevitable moment by moving it around a bit on my plate, and eating the chips and peas as slowly as possible.

The snag was we needed to be leaving for the cinema fairly soon. Everyone else finished theirs and left clean plates – so the spotlight was on me. It was dreadful. I just kept imagining how awful it would be actually putting that greasy, warm fish into my mouth. I was nearly sick just thinking about it. It was a *big* piece of fish – it seemed to occupy the whole plate – so I sliced it into two halves.

Fortunately, just as I was about to cut off a tiny forkful (I still feel sick thinking about it), Ros's mum and Ros got up and started to take a few plates and dishes through to the kitchen. I seized this opportunity.

I grabbed the two halves of fish in each hand – and *whoosh!* straight down into my trouser pockets.

'Ooh, good lad,' said Ros's mum. 'You gobbled that up quick. Would you like some more, there's just one piece left?'

'Er, no thanks,' I replied, 'we've got to get going or we'll be late for the pictures.'

Ros's dad had been with us all during the meal, but he hadn't said a word. However, he did raise the corner of his mouth slightly when I shook his hand on my way out.

We had to dash like mad to catch the bus to town. I never got a chance to offload my cargo. So when the conductor came round for the fares I had to rummage around in my pockets amongst the fried fish.

Needless to say the rest of the evening was ruined –
it was all a fishy, greasy, messy, smelly hell.

I had to abandon my date and flee home for a bath.

Patrick J., 53, technician

✽✽✽

It took me some time to summon up the courage to ask
Irene out for a quiet evening walk. I knew her mother
was apprehensive, because at the age of nineteen Irene
had led a very sheltered life. She had never before been
allowed out with a boy, her upbringing being very strict.

We lived on the edge of the countryside, and our
walk proceeded quietly and enjoyably. Before returning
home, we stopped at the village inn for a drink.

She downed three large port and lemons. I didn't
realize at the time that she had never been allowed to
drink, and was three parts gone as we walked home.

We had to cross a field and over a stile, where she
slipped and rolled into a cowpat.

I exclaimed 'Oh s✱✱✱' and tried to remove the stain
with paper, but only succeeded in making it look worse.
She in her condition found it all highly amusing.

We arrived back at her home, me in a high state of
trepidation, her laughing. Her mother immediately
realized with horror that her beloved, protected
daughter was not only several sheets to the wind, but
also covered with . . .

'What's that on your dress?' she cried. My date's
reply: 'Tom said it's s✱✱✱.'

I don't know how I managed it, but Irene and I have now been married over forty happy years.

Tom G., 64, caretaker

❧❧❧

WOMEN

Tottering down the road in my first pair of heels I feel the ache in my ankles and wonder how on earth I'll manage to walk back. Still, Ray might get us a taxi home.

I couldn't help seeing the tenner his dad slipped into his hand. Enough for that heart-shaped box of chocolates he promised me.

When we reach the Odeon I leave Ray to queue for tickets and swish my way to the Ladies. I fluff up my sugar-starched petticoat and slick another layer of Passion Pink over my lips. I daringly dab my cleavage with Fleur d'Amour. Oh, it'll be lovely sitting up there in the balcony WITH A BOY! Won't Jane O'Donnell be jealous!

I shrug off a sinking feeling as we follow the usherette to the very front row of the stalls. Soon it dawns on me that the only necking Ray has in mind is rubber-necking at the cowboy film he has pressurized me into seeing. As bullets whine and arrows fly Ray lifts the lid off my beautiful box. His jaws munch rhythmically and his arm dips and lifts like an automaton. I could be a Martian for all the notice he's taking of me.

165

My eyes sting with humiliation and my bladder makes insistent demands. Oh God, I'll have to go soon! My teenage Romeo, eyes firmly fixed on Gary Cooper, is totally unaware of my limping exit past my sniggering school friends.

My romantic illusions are in shreds, and it's only my first-ever date!

Nicola W., 54, ex-teacher

ॐ-ॐ-ॐ

I was twenty-one and a student nurse at the time. I hadn't known Geoff very long when he asked me out on this particular date.

He had a car. I don't remember the make or the model – but it wasn't warm, modern or the slightest bit comfortable. Nothing was arranged for this date. We drove around our (small) town the early part of the evening, with nowhere in mind.

So I suggested we go on to the nearest city, as there were more choices for entertainment there. Geoff drove through and nearly out of the city before turning into a deserted car park. Then he showed me the rolls of notes in his wallet.

It soon became obvious that he had no intention of spending any of it on me. For the next hour I sat in the car, in the cold and dark, listening to Geoff's renderings of Jim Reeves' songs. And boy, he counted himself as no mean streak with the talent.

When I managed to get a word in to say could we at

least think of getting something to eat, he said he'd parked opposite a chip shop deliberately. He left me to go into the shop (without asking what I'd like) and came back – would you believe – with ONE portion of fish and chips between us.

I was so glad to get back to the nurses' home.

And he had the unbelievable nerve to ring to ask for another date. A second round of cold, boredom and starvation? Thought I'd give it a miss.

Marjorie P., 57, aromatherapist

It was 1952 and my first trip abroad: a student tour to Vienna, Salzburg and Innsbruck. What could be more romantic?

One snag. More girls than boys. So I was thrilled when the hunky Welsh rugby player in the party paired off with me. What luck. But could I keep him with all those predatory females giving him the eye? I was determined he would be mine.

All was going well until that fateful walk in the moonlight. Together we strolled up the hill by the salt mines, the lights twinkling, the crickets singing, the balmy air casting a soothing breeze over our sun-baked skins.

There were seats built flush into the side of the hill, and as we sat down he put his arm around me. Suddenly, as we moved closer there was a terrible smell, and I felt a warm sticky substance seeping into my posterior. I leapt up to find . . .

I was covered in dog excrement.

Peeling my dress from my backside so that I could walk, we made our way back to the inn where I had to take a bath. When I had dressed again I looked out of my window. There was my Welsh rugby player walking off into the far distance with his arm round my best friend.

I returned home with a nice tan, but no man – and certainly no girlfriend.

Thelma I., 61, retired marketing manager

❦❦❦

He visited my office regularly, and appeared to be a very courtly gentleman. He was a friend of my boss, who had known him for years, so I readily accepted his invitation to go out for the evening.

We threaded our way through the traffic to the city centre, parked his swish car and spent a convivial half-hour in the bar of the plushest hotel. I rarely visited a city cinema. I was looking forward to it.

'Where are we going?' I asked animatedly.

'The Continental,' he said, in one of the main streets.

'Oh good,' I answered. Perhaps it would be some great foreign classic.

The lights were dimming as we entered and we fumbled to our seats in the dark. The film progressed very slowly for the first fifteen minutes. A girl in an office busy typing and answering the telephone – very mundane. Never mind, perhaps it would soon liven up.

I hadn't long to wait. To the sound of pounding tom-toms, the girl approached the man at a nearby desk, slowly unbuttoning her blouse and abandoning first her skirt, then her petticoat, her torso swaying sensuously to the heavy drum-beats.

For the first time I glanced around, noticing the predominance of middle-aged males in the audience. I was one of the few women there. I sank lower in my seat to avoid notice. I needn't have worried. Every eyeball was skewered to the strip-tease on the screen.

I wriggled with embarrassment next to the comparative stranger alongside me. My embarrassment turned to anger. Yes, he was a stranger. Fancy bringing me here on a first date. What did he think I was? As the girl on the screen prepared to discard the last remnant of clothing, I leapt up.

'I'm leaving,' I hissed into my companion's astonished face. 'I'm not sitting here watching that.' And, with all the outraged indignation of youth, I stalked out into the foyer.

Unfortunately, my grande dame exit was rather spoiled by having to go back in to borrow my bus fare home.

> *Brenda G., 65, retired local government*
> *administrative assistant*

The year, 1956. New boyfriend. Out to impress. Aged eighteen.

I had been asked by this super chap if I would like to drive to the nearest city to see a film.

Dressed up to kill. Five-inch heels on the new shoes. He collected me in his brand-new car, his pride and joy, and off we went. We had a lovely evening, everything went fine. I thought, yes, this is it.

I was rather shy, though, and I'd wanted to use the Ladies during the evening but did not like to say anything. On the drive home, I began to get desperate to use the loo. Finally, I could stand it no longer and asked if he could possibly stop the car as I needed the call of nature.

We were at that time in a country lane, so he stopped the car and I tottered off in my high heels down the road until I found a gate to a field. By this time it was nearly midnight, with no street lights.

Opening the gate I began to walk down into the field, but unfortunately failed to notice the pond.

I walked straight into it.

I emerged from the field an extremely bedraggled sight. I was covered in mud and slime up to my knees. I had also plunged my arms into the pond up to the elbows in an effort to retrieve my new shoes from the quagmire. I dripped and slimed my way back to my date's shiny new car.

He was not impressed.

He delved into the boot of his car and spread newspapers everywhere he could, wrapping them around my legs, arms and feet to keep his car clean.

In silence, we eventually got home. He never gave

me a chance to sully his car again.

Kathleen R., 55, company director

❦❦❦

When I was seventeen years old, during the early 1950s, I had my first date with Ken.

Ken was a policeman who lived in a single men's hostel, and the order of the day for dress was usually a trilby hat and a trench coat. Ken was no exception; he turned up wearing a wide-brimmed brown hat with a suit to match.

It was a fine summer's evening, lovely and warm without a breath of wind. We met outside a cafe in the small town where we both lived. It had very large windows, enabling everyone to see in and out easily.

We decided to have a cup of coffee and sat in a booth as we chatted. As we came out I had a strange feeling that something wasn't quite right. A feeling I didn't understand fully. Without dwelling on it, however, I pushed it out of my mind.

We took a bus to the nearest big town where we visited a restaurant, but as it was too crowded we didn't stay. Instead we returned to our own town, and as it was such a lovely evening had a leisurely stroll in the park.

Later Ken asked me if I would like a drink. As I had never been inside a public house before, I jumped at the chance. After all, I was only seventeen, and it felt awfully grown up. The place we went to was ever so posh, and I felt like a film star drinking my lemonade. No matter how I tried, however, that sensation came back, as if people were taking a second look at us.

Ken interrupted my thoughts. 'How about going to the Odeon to see what's on? If it's too late for tonight, we can always see what's coming.'

'OK,' I said, and off we went.

During the evening we had met quite a lot of friends and acquaintances of both of us. As we read the forthcoming attractions a uniformed policeman approached. After a brief introduction – another friend of Ken's – he apologized and took Ken a short distance away. My first thoughts were, 'Highly secret police work being discussed.' Then I saw it.

There was a condom on the back of Ken's hat.

Ken's face glowed so red and his eyes bulged so much I thought he was going to have a heart attack.

What would people think of me? I wondered in horror. The entire evening flashed through my mind, of all the friends I had met. No wonder we had been getting some strange looks.

A bus pulled into the stop, and without knowing where it was going I ran, jumped on, and was away.

Why had no one told him?

On second thoughts, who's going to approach and say 'Hey, you've got a condom pinned to the back of your hat.'

Not me, that's for certain.

Sarah W., 58, retired bookseller

8
'Young and hopeful,' eh?:
Women in the 1960s-1970s

1960s

I was seventeen – young and hopeful, and very impressionable. Caught up in the magic of those heady 'Swinging Sixties' years of instant 'pop stars', the Beatles, Cilla Black, mini skirts and Op-art earrings.

And HE had actually asked me out. That gorgeous bank clerk, whose amazing blue eyes had danced and teased me over the bank counter for weeks. He had not only asked me out, but out 'to dinner', at the most sumptuous restaurant in town – all soft lights, candles in wine bottles, and cosy little alcove tables for two with deep-buttoned velvety sofas.

Oh gosh! I'd found my El Dorado, my knight in shining armour – it was going to be a date made in heaven. Panic! What should I wear? Something stunning ... this would take some thinking about, in fact the strategy and planning of the Normandy landing. This was to be no ordinary date, oh no! This was going to be special, a night to remember.

I could hardly wait for the afternoon to pass, so I could get home and sink into a bubble bath of perfume and savour the excitement yet to come. Yes! The purple mini skirt – oh and the purple and black crochet top, black fishnet tights, and my new knee-length black shiny boots! (How my mother *ever* let me out of the house in such an outfit is to this day still a mystery to me!) There I was, surveying my image in the mirror – 'perfection'. Well, not really *perfection*, but not bad, not bad at all . . .

Seven-thirty! There, at the appointed time, outside the restaurant waiting, was my 'Grecian god'. And I, strolling up to him tossing my Silvikrin-advert hair, would be his 'Diana', or Artemis, or everything!

The meal was divine – we wined and dined, chatted and laughed. It was all going like clockwork. I felt wonderful, he had even said I looked beautiful (thank goodness I'd given myself an egg white face pack) – what more could I ask?

Then he asked if I'd like to walk along the river. Being June, the weather would be warm and sultry still. My heart pounding, little butterflies leaping in my stomach, I got up from my seat and felt giddy with desire (or it may have been the wine).

We made our way out of the alcove and across the room. It seemed that my happiness was infectious, for smiling looks followed us as we left.

But wait, something else was following us.

I turned, a little uneasily.

A thread from my fishnet tights had wound itself around the deep buttons in the sofa, and had unravelled itself to follow me around several tables and chairs!

There was 'Diana', entwined and engulfed in embarrassment, while the 'Grecian god' collapsed into gales of 'rugby-like' laughter as he wrestled with his multi-purpose Swiss army knife to release me from my stringy prison.

Once home (walk along the river hastily abandoned), the remains of the tights were binned.

And so, sadly, was the romance!

Laura C., 45, building society clerk

❧❧❧

This wasn't so much a date from hell as from purgatory or even limbo. We were both fifteen and he had just left a seminary, having decided that he didn't after all want to be a priest. I should have realized that it might not be the most scintillating evening ever when his friend asked for the date on his behalf, because he was too shy to approach me himself.

He met me from the bus, we walked to the cinema, queued for tickets, sat through the trailers, two films (they still had a B-feature in those days) and an interval, walked back to the bus stop and waited for my bus.

All without either of us saying one word.

Of course, after the first half-hour or so it became impossible to break the silence, even if either of us had been able to think of anything to say.

What amazes me, looking back, is that we had several more dates (with some help from his friend). This truly was the triumph of hope over experience as the results were much the same. We had about a six-word courtship before deciding to give our vocal

175

chords some exercise elsewhere.

Of course, I put the whole thing down to *his* shyness as I knew that I was – in all other circumstances – a very talkative person. For obvious reasons, I've no idea what he made of it all.

Still, Trappist monasteries are always on the lookout for recruits.

Daphne H., 44, lecturer

ꝏ-ꝏ-ꝏ

I was nineteen when I spotted this handsome hunk in my local working man's club. I feasted my eyes on him all night, but no glance from him came my way until it was nearly closing time. Our eyes locked together and he actually blushed. I didn't. Well, I was intent on snaring him and I felt the signals were appropriate. Sure enough, when I headed for the door, he was waiting.

Close up he was handsomer than from my seat four rows away. I smiled my most sensual smile. Oh my heart was beating so fast. Would he ask me out the following week? My mate was beckoning me to run for the bus – but no, I wanted to hear his voice. So I began the sort of conversation that in hindsight verged on the ridiculous. But I persevered, and eventually he replied to the usual banalities of a teenager well smitten. His tonal qualities matched his looks and I fair swooned inside.

After ten minutes I guess I got the message that he

wasn't going to walk me home, but he did intimate that he would be back the following Friday to see the popular 'turn' I was a fan of too.

All the way home I nattered on about my 'hunk' and how I must go to C & A and treat myself to the latest craze. My mate told me off at my constant references to my 'dreamboat' and we parted on acrimonious terms. I reckoned she was jealous.

All that week I was on cloud nine, and I had this scenario in my head that on our first date he would take me to a 'posh' place and wine and dine me with no expense spared. I didn't earn much, and for that matter I had never 'gone places', so here was I visualizing all kinds of good times.

It seemed to drag to that Friday night. I felt a million dollars as I swanned into the club kitted out in my latest 'sweater girl' gear: tight split skirt, equally tight jumper, elastic belt to emphasize my then trim waistline, sheer seamed stockings and stiletto high-heels. A fortune, that had cost me. But with my blonde pageboy hairstyle, I felt he would fall for me in a trice.

All I wanted was for him to walk in and claim me for his date that night. Two hours later he turned up. I was well oiled by this time and full of alcoholic bravado. I waved frantically at him and he winked at me and gave me a flashing smile. I started grinning like a cat that had got all the cream. I sidled out of my seat and slinked over to him at the bar. Soon I was sloshing down more 'best bitter' and giving out the vibes.

Closing time came amazingly quickly and soon we

were heading for the cool night air. He took my arm and said intimately that he would take me to the bus stop and that he would meet me during the week. Even in my befuddled state I felt elated at his words, and as I waved to him from the bus I felt the inward thrill of 'getting' such a hunk.

I dreamed such dreams that night.

Turning up at the city centre to wait for him was agony, as I began to feel that he might have only been playing up to my attentions. People sailed by glancing at me waiting on the corner, and as I started to feel the urge to hide, I espied my dreamboat coming towards me.

He greeted me warmly and said we'd get a taxi to this place he knew. I was just a jelly mess quaking at the thought of his amorous attentions later. I still couldn't really believe that I had 'pulled' so handsome a fella!!

We alighted at a well-lit place that was obviously another working man's club. I felt a slight tremor of disappointment. My visions of living it up had already diminished, and I noticed on the way that he didn't say much. On entering the club he asked me what I'd like to drink. I replied 'Gin and orange, please.' He said 'Eh?' So I repeated my choice.

He sauntered off to the bar, pulling out a purse to pay for the drinks. My hunk lessened a bit in my eyes. I hated men who carried their money around like that – it just didn't seem manly in those days of my rock 'n' roll youth.

He came back with the drinks and there we sat.

And sat and sat.

No words came out of his mouth.

Not a single one.

I gabbled on, thinking, 'He'll come out of his shell any minute.' But no, nothing at all emitted from his beautifully shaped lips.

My Adonis, the one I'd yearned for for days and days, was revealed as a total bore. Perhaps he thought if he talked as *well* as looking gorgeous it would all be too much for me.

Gail T., 51, part-time student in computer studies

❦❦❦

I was seventeen years of age, newly employed with a large firm and being shown the ropes by a woman who had a single son whom she doted on. Being boy-friendless, it didn't take much persuasion from my immediate boss for me to accept a blind date with her offspring.

He duly arrived at my parental doorstep, and was driving his father's car. I was suitably impressed at this early stage of the date. Dressed in a mini skirt and high stiletto shoes (high fashion of the period), I carefully settled myself into the passenger seat, looking forward to the coming afternoon.

We parked by the seaside. I was then escorted to a silly little rowing boat which I very bravely entered. With me clinging to the sides, he manoeuvred it out to a slightly larger one which he called a yacht. I was appropriately petrified, being only able to swim a few widths of a pool and not having been supplied

179

with a life jacket. Or common sense.

The wind sprang up violently, the waves lashed the sides of the 'yacht'. I was commanded to sit down as I was in danger of capsizing us. My shoes were a mess, my skirt appeared to have risen to my thighs, my heart thudded uncontrollably and tears were in danger of cascading down my cheeks. In fact, my cool was totally lost and I vowed there and then never to go on another blind date.

While feeling completely sodden and bereft, he accused me of calling another boy 'Darling' in his mother's presence – she'd told him. I couldn't deny it.

We did eventually arrive at my doorstep, me feeling bedraggled and completely unrepentant, him – as if he had the right on first acquaintance – really mad at me.

I married the 'Darling' instead.

Mary W., 46, receptionist

🐾🐾🐾

I was forty-five, and just coming back to life again after being widowed twelve months previously. I was fortunate in having a full-time career which kept me busy. My friends, however, thought it was time I began accepting social invitations.

One day a friend telephoned. She and her husband were short of a partner for a business friend aged about fifty for an evening out in a week's time. Would I make the numbers up?

Well, I had never had a blind date, but I didn't think

I was too old to start. So I said yes. Henry would call for me at seven-thirty the following Wednesday. But, as I lived in a remote part of the county, he would telephone during the week for directions.

Henry did phone, several times, and there were long conversations. He sounded so nice, and I was getting more and more excited at the thought of meeting him. At one point, he asked me how I would describe myself. Was I modern? I said I would have to ask my 22-year-old son. He said, 'Well Mum, I would tell him you are modern-ish.'

So on Wednesday week, after deciding that I had better put on my shortest dress, I contemplated false eyelashes but rejected the idea as I didn't think I would get them on right. Five minutes before the deadline, after spending an hour on my modern-ish appearance, I was ready. I thought I was perhaps rather too dolled up, but perhaps Henry would approve.

Now it so happened, that at approximately seven-thirty, my spinster neighbour – who was sixty and very definitely not modern-ish – chose to call on me. In doing so, she also chose to take her time walking up the drive and inspecting my roses.

I was looking out of my window, and I saw a car draw up outside my front gate. The car stopped for a moment. The driver took one quick look at my neighbour and, with foot hard down on the accelerator, shot out of my life for ever.

Nora P., 70, retired catering officer

❦❦❦

Should I? Shouldn't I?

I stared at myself in the mirror. My nose was not only red, sore and peeling from constant blowing, but I swear it was twice its normal size. But boy I wanted to go. It would be the party of the term, no, the year. Perhaps the party of my life. Pete had asked me. But I still felt terrible.

For the best part of two weeks I had not even been to art college, let alone out of an evening. Pete was unbelieving. His fragile male ego was certain I was making it up. I'd kept putting him off, he thought, getting the landlady to lie for me. We had only been going out for a couple of months and he was keen. I was keen, but not with 'flu. So there were two reasons for saying yes. One: to convince Pete I was still really interested. Two: who wants to miss the invitation-only, bouncers-booked party of a lifetime?

I scrounged around in the bottom of my bag for four pennies, went to the call box and made an appointment with the college doctor. Pills, I needed pills, then I could go. Might even feel actually well. After all, two days of intensive pill-swallowing would precede the party.

Prescription filled. The chemist gave me a glass of water in the shop. I took the first dose before the label had stuck to the bottle.

I asked for four pennies in the change and went to call Pete. He needed to know. If I wasn't coming, he was sure as hell going to take someone else. He would not miss a party he had been instrumental in organizing. He could not arrive alone. Unheard of.

I rang him at work. 'Hold the line please.' I tapped my feet impatiently in the smelly red box. Had every man and his dog used this as a urinal? Suddenly I did not care. I could smell! I could actually smell urine. I must be getting better.

I had had no taste or sense of smell for ages. I brightened, only to be told that Pete was out and uncontactable. I was left looking at the handset as if this black hunk of plastic had just slapped me in the face.

Curses. But if I could smell again, I could go round to his digs and leave a note. I waited, in the wind which I swear only blows at bus stops, and got the bus. An hour later, back in my digs, I made myself an enormous mug of hot tea. I proceeded to ignore the fact that I had started sweating like a pig. When I began to shake too, I swallowed two more pills. The box said not to be taken with alcohol. That was all right, I was drinking tea. Two days. I only had to hang in there for two days.

The landlady woke me. 'Pete on the phone for you.' I crawled to the phone. We fixed for him to collect me about nine on the Saturday. He said he had to be there reasonably early to let the beer settle. (Bit late Pete, I thought, as beer needs at least a day to settle. But what can you do?) He had the boot that would take the nine-gallon firkin. Most of these parties started after the pubs had shut, lessening the load on the hosts to provide alcohol.

As we finished the call he said, 'New rule: this is a three-pieces-of-clothing party as you know. But we all decided that a pair of something counts as two. So a pair of jeans counts as two items.' I see, I said to myself, even less to rip off later. 'S'pose that doesn't apply to a pair of knickers, does it?'

''Course it does!' he said and was gone.

Actually, come Saturday I did feel a lot better. My best friend Viv called to check if I was OK for the party. I said, try to keep me away. 'What you wearing?' I asked. She said her new jeans had shrunk to fit nicely after several evenings wearing them in the bath. She would put one of her boyfriend's football shirts on top. 'Not very dressy, Viv?' Going out with Pete these past few weeks had led me to believe a dress was the only possible route. A dress, my long Biba dress and a pair of knickers it would be.

Saturday evening at eight fifty-five, I swallowed another dose to be sure, just as the Ford Cortina screeched to a halt at the gate. I'd made it.

We took the beer to the farmhouse five of the blokes on Pete's course rented. He set it on blocks in the kitchen. Looking about I hardly recognized the place. All the furniture had been stacked away. Most of the light bulbs had gone too. Soon it would be full of half-drunk students. Pot-smoking, beer-drinking students for the Rave of the Year.

It was after the third half-pint of suspiciously (and unsurprisingly) cloudy beer, but only our second dance, that I began to feel awful. I felt hot but I did not want to have to go home. So I dived for the pills and knocked back two more for good measure. I was here and I was jolly well going to be here for when they judged the best-dressed person.

Best dressed seemed synonymous with least dressed.

Rob had just run through the ground floor naked. Things were hotting up in a way that actually began to concern me just a teensy-weensy bit. I leant against the wall and tried not to hear Colin, my best friend's fella, negotiating an hour's use of one of the bedrooms with one of Pete's mates.

Pete shoved another refilled tankard in my hand and suggested we took a spell outside. 'Going outside' meant a grope in my day. Definitely preferable to a bed. I had absolutely no intention of sleeping with Mr Cortina this night, however much he thought his ownership of said car gave him the right to get inside my knickers.

It was my way. It had happened before. A rush of fresh air and I feel decidedly drunk all at once. Impossible, really, though. I was only sipping my second pint.

But faint I felt. Very woozy in fact. I stumbled. Caught the hem of my Biba dress and virtually fell into Pete's willing arms. He, I have to say, was not drunk. He was very in control. He was also delighted things were obviously going just according to plan.

He fumbled me back upright. Hands freely exploring the full geography of my continents. Seeking only now to dive into my seas, both with tongue and the rapidly growing member that thrust between us.

I swooned again. The fool actually believed I was overcome with passion. Limp in his arms I was bending to his will. Like a lily in the breeze. Mumbles I recall were about 'bed', 'all right', 'got a Johnny'.

Then all I see is sixteenth-century farmhouse ceiling. The plaster cracks above me are going out of focus.

185

My boyfriend undresses by the light of a bedside lamp. I lift my head from the pillow to take in the panorama as if it is the last view of this world I shall ever see. Already I am feeling quite separate from this body of mine. But eyes see the chair shoved up tight under the door handle to keep out the hordes. Oh good, no audience, I giggle inwardly.

The floor is covered with piles of duffle coats and scarves hastily removed from the bed in which I now lie. The curtains, heavy velvet, are pulled as if in haste, for a 'V' of night sky still winks at me directly ahead. If 'they' climbed the tree in the yard they could watch still, I think. Then I swing my head to see Pete naked, with one of the largest erections I have ever seen. But to be honest, I have not seen many.

He is cursing as he fumbles with the rubber. His mother, if she's like mine, would be saying, more haste less speed. No, my mother would be saying nothing of the sort! She would be horrified. Her little girl being seduced by this wicked man.

Her little girl was for once perfectly at one with her mother. No way was this going to happen without me being conscious. My virginity – my long-held (for art college) virginity – was not going tonight.

I managed a weak 'No' as he slid in between the heavy covers beside me. He looked into my eyes, saw the light in them go out and echoed my 'No' with a groan of disappointment. Even Mr Cortina was not a necrophiliac. He too wanted me conscious. Apparently he tried to bring me round for some time. Then he actually had to admit this was serious.

Viv was prised from the bedroom down the corridor.

She panicked. Viv does. 'Col, call an ambulance!' She told Pete how ill I had been, and about the drugs. Handbag revealed the offending bottle. There, too, the legend 'Not to be taken with alcohol'.

Before the ambulance arrived, the police did. Nothing to do with me, actually. A noise complaint from a neighbour with 'student party', 'way past midnight', 'naked people', 'probably drugs' being bandied about.

So the police variously searched the place or stood in the kitchen supping from the firkin. The music was turned down. The word had already spread that Pete's bird had O.D.ed on drugs and that was what this was all about.

Amazing how a rowdy, boisterous crowd of 'fearless' students can cower into embarrassed wimps, all disclaiming rapidly that any of this has anything to do with them and trying hard not to look too out of their heads. This type of party-goer calls the police 'pigs' by day and then sucks up to them by night with beer, while Jimmy flushes best Lebanese red down the loo. (Fortunately the police had come too late to find the bloke lying on the floor, twisting a black rubber doorstop and crying 'I can't get this f***ing door to open.')

I come round. The first life sign to return to me is sound. I hear sirens. Then I pick out human voices. Concerned human voices. Subsequently I begin to hear actual words, as if my ability to hear has come back to me from a long, long way away. Then I put faces to the voices. Pete looking down into my face. 'Thank God, Kath, I thought you'd gone.' Then a police face. 'What's your name, Miss?' 'What . . . er . . . Kath. Why?'

There is an influx of two men and a stretcher. The

room is bursting at the seams. 'You OK, love?' The ambulance crew take over. 'Can you get on to the stretcher.' 'Why?' The only word I feel able to say. 'We want to get you to hospital, love.' His face disappears. But his voice continues, 'Anyone know what she's on?'

While the emergency services debate their various attitudes to the word 'drugs' – the ambulance crew want to rush me to hospital, the police are excited at the thought of prosecuting me – I go into self-preservation mode. Prison looms before me. Parents visiting me shame-faced and tearful. College principal, arm outstretched and pointing, banishing me like some Oliver Twist from the college gates. God, this is hell!

''Scuse me.' I tug on the nearest official sleeve. 'Do I have to go to casualty?' 'No.' The word is like music in my ears. Images of hell recede. 'Then I don't want to. I'll be OK. I feel an absolute fool. I've had 'flu. I'm on antibiotics. Show him, Pete.' I wave a naked arm in the direction of the wimp in the corner. 'Didn't realize no alcohol meant no alcohol.'

I whimpered a bit. 'That's all. I'm sorry, I know we've wasted your time.'

Pete produced the capsules. They were passed round the whole room. Police, ambulance crew, I swear they all looked knowingly, as if they could confirm without benefit of doctorate or pharmaceutical training that these drugs, these pink and green bombs, were harmless. We all colluded in ending the whole sorry episode here and now. The room emptied like a snake unfurling and slipping away into the rocks. An awkward silence fell on the room, now that Pete and I were left alone.

Pete said, 'All you had to say was, "I don't want to sleep with you tonight," you know.'

Kath D., 45, therapist

ళళళ

1970s

I had one evening date with a new boyfriend, which could only be described as a bit of heaven and a bit of hell.

We were both about seventeen at the time. My mum and dad were going out for the evening and so, for the first time ever, we had the place to ourselves for a while. We were going to sit and watch television – we said. Anyway, we soon got around to kissing and cuddling. Then one thing led to another, and we ended up making love on the carpet in front of the settee.

That was the 'heaven' bit (or near enough). Then we heard footsteps coming down the path. It was mum and dad, back early!

A mad scramble to get our clothes back on and try to pretend nothing had happened. Just as they came in through the front door, we plonked ourselves on the settee and frantically tried to look interested in the telly.

When my boyfriend stood up (he was quite well-mannered) he (and I) noticed, to our utter horror, the used durex lying on the carpet. Bob quickly stepped on it to hide it from the scavenging eyes of my mum and dad.

After standing there a while, Bob said that he'd have to be going now. No, he couldn't stay for a cuppa, thank you. We both felt dread – how were we going to get him out without giving the game away? My parents would have hit the roof – and probably me and Bob as well!

Bob started sidling slowly and shiftily towards the door – he was dragging the durex along the carpet under his foot! My parents started to stare at him, clearly intrigued by his strange movements. I was literally dumbstruck with horror at the thought of what would surely now be soon revealed.

Fortunately, thank God, Bob managed to make it out to the front door without letting the durex slip from under his foot. But it was ten minutes of hell – from mum and dad coming in to Bob's exit.

Afterwards, when Bob had gone, my parents remarked on what a nice young man he seemed to be. 'It's a shame about his leg, though,' said my dad. 'A motorbike accident, was it?'

Annette S., 40, nurse

🎵🎵🎵

I was smitten the first time I laid eyes on Jake. He was a Hell's Angel – the leader of the pack.

I was all fired up after spending the past hour dancing to heavy rock when Jake rode into the club car park with his biker entourage. The noise was ear-splitting as they revved the machines, grouping together in a circle of studded black leather. The men looked wickedly frightening. Some rode alone, while others had leather-clad girlfriends sporting vast expanses of leg and long wind-whipped hair.

Jake rode alone. As I watched in awe I made up my mind that I would be one of their pack. I would ride with Jake.

Inside the club the atmosphere prickled with anticipation as the bikers parted the crowd and Jake caught my eye. I loved him at first sight. He was good-looking in a mean sort of way, he was scary and his mates jumped when he spoke. I spent the evening in his arms, chatting, listening to the heavy beat, aware of his *maleness*.

When the music died there was talk amongst the pack about going on to a nightclub. My heart raced with excitement. Jake held me close as we headed for the bikes and as I mounted his machine he took hold of my hands and placed them tightly around his waist. We roared into the darkness. I was high on love, exhilarated by the speed but, to my surprise, with a wave, Jake split from the rest of the pack.

I found myself on my own doorstep minutes later.

Great. Riding with the leader of the pack for about 500 yards.

'But I thought we were going to a nightclub?' I asked. I desperately didn't want the night to end.

Jake, a man of few words, stroked his hand down my cheek and smiled. 'You're just a baby – see you tomorrow.'

I was so disappointed. That night set a precedent. It was the first of many, but Jake always took me home early and returned to the pack. I was consumed with the desire to find out where they went, and after a while I spent a whole evening begging Jake to let me stay with them. (I reckoned it was time, as I was his girl, wasn't I?)

With a shrug he finally submitted. The pack was heading for *his* place that night. I was thrilled. Finally I had a real date with Jake, not just hanging around the club.

Jake flicked on the flat's lights and headed for the fridge. He had just grasped a six-pack when the bedroom door creaked open. A yawning woman emerged. Jake's real and obviously live-in girlfriend. She was huge, she was tattooed, she was the biker from hell and she was after my blood. Jake simpered beside her while I fled before she rearranged my face.

I was devastated, wounded to the core. But not as wounded as Jake was when I next saw him at the club nursing two black eyes and a broken nose.

Somehow he had just lost his credibility.

Beverley J., 38, housewife/student

❦❦❦

In 1974 I was dating an Arab doctor. Although he had rooms within the main hospital building, we always met outside. We would go for a drive and drinks; fruit juice, as he was strictly opposed to alcohol.

I felt that we were two very attracted people who were drawing slowly, teasingly, towards the 'grand passion'.

One Saturday afternoon he telephoned to ask if, instead of meeting him outside, I would go to the main reception desk. As they bleeped him, I felt quite important and more excited than usual; the 'power is an aphrodisiac' syndrome, I supposed. I knew that this would be the first time we would go to bed together.

Once in the bedroom, I was rather puzzled when he asked me to lie with my head at the bottom of the bed, facing the headboard. As we made love, missionary position, he began to emit the oddest cursing noises in Arabic. (Was it the Arab equivalent of 'oh God, oh God,' I wondered?)

Suddenly he just jumped up, arms flailing, shrieking incomprehensibly, leaving me in mid-sigh, utterly startled! I turned over on to my stomach to see what on earth was going on.

Unbeknown to me, he had been watching the television at the end of the bed, sound down. The programme was extended news coverage of the Arab-Israeli war.

Something critical had apparently happened mid-bonk.

Rita K., 43, nurse

I was eighteen, just gone up to university from a provincial convent school, shy and extremely short-sighted.

Through vanity I attended the Freshers Ball without my glasses. All I could tell about the boy who asked me to dance was that he was very tall, but he was pleasant enough to talk to.

He plodded along beside me on the way back to the halls of residence and my friend, following behind, thought we looked more like a policeman accompanying a suspect to the station than a romantic couple. However, his farewell words to me on the doorstep were that he would dream about me and would take me to the cinema the following day.

The next day he escorted me to a local cinema that was showing *Diary of a Nymphomaniac*. I still wasn't wearing my glasses but the dialogue was explicit enough. I was too shy to walk out but was shocked into silence for the rest of the evening. I never saw him again after that and still don't know what he looked like.

When I got back, I poured out my tale of woe about the disgusting film to my sympathetic friend. The next day she was mysteriously absent from her room. I later found out she'd gone to see the film.

Suzie T., 39, bilingual secretary

❦❦❦

After a student demo in London, me and my friend Lizzie decided to spend a night on the tiles instead of getting the coach back to college in the sticks.

We went for a cheap meal in a Soho wine bar, where we met François. Conversation was limited since he spoke as little English as we did French, and his platforms and curly perm were at least half a decade out of date even by our provincial standards. Still, we were in the mood for adventure and hoped he might lead us to it.

Jesus Christ Superstar was on at the theatre, and on François's recommendation we bought standby seats for the upper circle. When we were leaving I dropped my scarf and it lodged on a set of lights a few feet below the gallery. Before we could stop him François was in death-defying action, dangling over the balcony to retrieve it while Lizzie and I clung to his legs, horrified.

Things fell a bit flat after that as we'd spent all our money and François didn't have any either. Deciding to start for home, we said goodbye to him at Piccadilly Circus. Thirty minutes later, alighting from the tube at Euston, we were less than enchanted to see him step on to the platform a few carriages down, grinning sheepishly.

He was very emotional when our train arrived, saying we were the first two friends he'd made in England. Partly out of sympathy, more out of fear that he might attempt to come back with us there and then, we promised to meet him in our town the following week.

In the course of telling friends about the evening, we couldn't resist taking a few liberties with the truth, particularly where François was concerned. We even managed to convince ourselves he wasn't as undesirable as we'd thought and, on the appointed night, curiosity led us to the station to see if he'd turned up.

He had. Simultaneously catching a glimpse of beige flares and flashing gold neck chain, we made to escape. But François was already hastening across the concourse, arms thrown wide to embrace us.

There was no alternative but to make the best of things, and after a few drinks we were marching through the streets to a nightclub, singing the 'Marseillaise' at the tops of our voices.

Inside we were mortified to meet several people we knew from college. They watched with evident amusement as François cornered me on the dance floor, his face glistening with sweat, limbs flailing in energetic homage to 'Saturday Night Fever'.

On my way back from a well-earned breather in the Ladies, I looked in vain for Lizzie, eventually spotting her hand clawing desperately at the air while the rest of her was pinned against the wall by a determined Gallic snogger.

At two a.m. we did the dishonourable thing: scarpered. As we made it to the exit I looked back to see François, still grooving away, quite oblivious to his abandonment.

Walking back to the hall of residence we laughed spitefully about his awfulness. Inside, I think we both felt just a bit ashamed about being unfair and the way we'd handled it all.

François rose like a phoenix, however. A few days later we received a postcard, sent to our college faculty from London. It read: 'I love both. Alas, I cannot choose between.'

Jenny T., 34, newspaper copytaker

༺༅༅༅༅

I was young, confident, popular. My best friend was in the clutch of her first love affair. I was in between my first and second. Dennis, her boyfriend, was a div; in today's language, a dork, a nerd. Weedy, wore suits – SUITS! – with Mum-chosen ties . . . in the 1970s?!

'Please,' she pleaded with me, 'please, Julie, Dennis says he's really good-looking.'

She wanted to make up a foursome for his firm's Christmas dinner dance. I agreed, in the end, to make her happy – after all, she was my best friend. I consoled myself that surely no one could be worse than Dennis.

Karen and I arrived at the designated pub, resplendent in body-hugging Chelsea Girl. Dennis and she greeted each other with suppressed passion, and I was left to scan the room for Eric, my date for the evening.

'Julie, meet Eric.' Dennis beamed, I stared. Eric equalled my 5ft 5in height. To me he was utterly unattractive and, as a final touch, came complete with a straggled black moustache. His tie was a nightmare of what I thought were soup stains.

Throughout the meal he stroked my neck, my arms, dropped his fork and trailed his wet moustache across my bare shoulder as he bent to pick it up. Karen shot me despairing and guilt-ridden looks as later, on the dance floor, he crushed me to him and buried his mouth in my neck, his hands rubbing, groping, slithering.

Later, in the Ladies, I begged Karen to take a taxi home with me, but she didn't want to offend her Love.

Eric drove home, the other two necking in the back, me crushing my body into the passenger door in an attempt to evade the slippery knee grasp of my date. To my horror, he dropped them off at Karen's home first.

I had to add twenty pounds of muscle to my skinny father and an extra, older, brother to my family to dissuade him from the local Lovers Lane.

He stopped at the top of my road.

I went for the door handle, garbling thanks and goodbyes. He leaned across, pulled a lever, my seat back dropped flat and so did he – on top of me!

I persevered with the door handle manoeuvre, it opened, I wriggled, thrust, and rolled on to the pavement. I came up running.

I left one of my tasteful platform shoes, Cinderella-like, behind me.

He called me but I was in the front door to the sanctuary of home before he could move from the car.

'Did you have a nice night, dear?' asked my mother.

'Wonderful,' I replied.

Julie K., 39, picture editor

9
'Fate plays gooseberry':
Circumstances, accidents and interference

I'd met this chap when I was out horseriding in the park. We fancied each other, he was terribly rich (I was poor as a church mouse at the time), and he invited me to Paris for the weekend. Hell of a first date, I thought. I'll go.

The tube was terribly slow to Heathrow, and I thought 'My God, I'm going to miss the plane.' We'd arranged to meet at the ticket desk, but I decided to go straight to the plane or it'd be too late.

I sat in Club class, he wasn't in his seat, the doors shut and we were off, me muttering 'Oh no, oh *no*.'

He, meanwhile, was waiting at the ticket desk. Woman at desk: 'She *can't* have got on, sir.' Wait, wait, wait. Him: 'Please check again for me.' Her: 'Well, er, yes, she does appear to be on the plane.'

So he got the next flight.

I reckoned I'd been stood up. He'd told me that he had booked a suite at the very swish Hotel X. I thought well, I can't go there in case he hasn't booked it after all. So I checked into what was probably the most grotty hotel in Paris. A honeymoon resort for cockroaches.

I decided to try to ring the swish hotel, just in case. My French isn't too bad and I managed to get through.

He was there! Oh joy! Oh wonderful!

But now I had a hotel bill to pay, and no money (he'd given me the air ticket). I explained my story to the manager, and he let me off the bill. *Yes* to Anglo-French relations.

So off I went to Hotel X. It was the most beautiful, elegant place. He'd booked dinner in the hotel restaurant, which cost the earth. 'Have what you want,' he said. I did. Caviar, champagne, oysters.

He said, 'Let's go to bed.'

We went upstairs. He started the overtures. 'Darling,' he said. 'Darling,' I said. 'I'm going to be sick.'

'No you're not,' he said. 'It's just panic.'

I said 'No, I'm going to be sick,' and fled to the bathroom. Allergic to oysters.

He held my head all night while I threw up.

After that, passion died.

The next day he took me shopping. I could barely walk. He took me to another wonderful restaurant. I couldn't eat a mouthful. It was opposite a row of the most fabulous department stores. He had his credit cards at the ready. I couldn't stagger far enough to get through the doors. I simply couldn't face it.

In the end, he bought me a handbag at the airport.

So I'd thrown up the entire night, couldn't eat the heavenly food, and *no shopping* at his expense. I couldn't have anything. I was so upset.

I had to stop going riding. I might have bumped into him.

Frances D., 34, businesswoman

200

❦❦❦

I was unsure at first if he was actually asking me out. I thought he was trying to sell me tickets. Even when I realized it was an invitation, I knew I was first – or even second – reserve. Still, newly single, I intended playing the field and thought, so what? Even as a reserve, I'll get to see Status Quo, and eat out into the bargain.

'Will it entail much walking?' I checked the important details. Stiletto heels can be debilitating. 'None,' he assured me, sounding more certain of that than he had about actually inviting me.

So I planned my outfit. Silk shirt, body stocking, and I'd borrow my friend Lynda's jacket. 'We'll take taxis everywhere,' he'd said, and I was impressed. Here was chivalry in its rarest form, even if it had come my way by default. Oh yes, and we were going with two of his friends.

So, newly henna-ed hair straightened to perfection, face painted and outfit donned, I was collected. So far so good. He was in a leather jacket and the other couple were in hiking boots and Barbour jackets. Fleetingly, I did wonder if they – the Eskimo brigade – knew something I didn't.

The concert was fun, though, even if I was now temporarily deaf in one ear. Arm about my shoulders, he guided me protectively towards the exit and the one and only telephone kiosk, where, it seemed, everyone who had been at the concert was queuing to phone for a taxi. And this was where the real problems began.

He decided that we should start walking and flag down a cab en route. Once outdoors, the reason for the popularity of the phone kiosk became clear. The heavens had opened, the wind howled and even the woman from the other couple complained of bruising from the hailstones.

'We'll take a short cut across the field,' he decided, and soon I had even bigger problems. Friend Lynda was wanting to wear this jacket tomorrow and I had the distinct feeling that by then it would be at least two sizes smaller. Three-quarter sleeves are, sadly, no longer trendy.

I then lost a boot heel in the mud. He hoisted me back up comfortingly. I'd delivered 12,000 newspapers to buy these boots!

Eventually at the restaurant, I surveyed the damage. Once devoid of Barbours, his friends were fine. So, too, he and his leather. Lynda's jacket, on the other hand, was stuck fast to a now transparent silk shirt, shirt to body stocking and body stocking to me. The only respectable, fully functioning part of me were my nipples, which somehow seemed to be more than usually prominent. In any other situation, I might have looked erotic. But steaming profusely by the radiator, mascara streaked and hair shrivelling, I resembled a toilet brush rather than Ursula Andress emerging nipples first from the warm Adriatic.

I asked for the hottest Indian dish, and for the first time he looked quite concerned. I didn't explain that I was thinking of sitting in it, not eating it. My boots were now the consistency of the newsprint I had delivered in their honour, and stood about as much chance of warming my feet as the Arctic did of melting.

Several Comforts of a Southern nature later, I had mellowed a little. My ear was beginning to function again and I made a few resolutions. Next time I am the substitute, or even the First Reserve, I will ensure my presence at the venue, but make damn sure I don't actually take to the field.

Ellie S., 38, community worker

❦❦❦

I had been madly and passionately in love with David since I was ten years old. He, however, was a sophisticated sixteen-year-old at the time and never so much as glanced at me. All through my teens I worshipped him from afar, but just as I began to develop interesting curves he took off for distant parts.

In due course, I met and married someone else but the marriage was short-lived. By the time I heard that David was back in town I was single again.

On the pretext of returning some books I had borrowed from him years before, I rang David and was thrilled when he asked me out for a meal at a local hotel. I had my hair cut in a new and exciting style, spent a whole month's wages on sexy lingerie, a new dress and a killer perfume and, with my Dutch cap tucked in my handbag 'just in case,' I set off to meet him knowing I looked fantastic.

We met in the hotel reception, and the mutual attraction was instant and electric. As soon as he took me into his arms for a 'hello' hug I was so aroused that I almost fainted, and I could feel that he was in a similar state. Without a thought for the people around us, he gave me a long, lingering kiss. Then as we finally broke apart, flushed and trembling, he took my hand, looked into my eyes and whispered 'Shall I book a room?'

We went through the motions of eating our meal, all the while holding hands. As soon as we could decently escape, we went upstairs to the bedroom where we began undressing each other the moment the door had closed behind us. After about an hour of kissing, stroking and fondling, I suddenly realized that my Dutch cap was still in my handbag.

With great difficulty, we stopped our passionate foreplay and David went into the bathroom to give me a moment's privacy to insert it. Lying on the bed, I carefully smeared both sides with spermicidal jelly. I was just about to put it in place when it shot from my shaking fingers, flew into the air and stuck firmly to the bedroom ceiling.

Two hours later, when it finally succumbed to the effects of gravity and fell down again, David and I were lying on the bed in fits of hysterical laughter. We tried to make love again several times that night, but every time one of us would get an attack of the giggles and be unable to continue.

All this happened twelve years ago. David and I became very good friends and still see each other to this day, even though we have both since married other people. Neither of our partners knows why, on occasion, we can't look at each other without giggling . . .

Kathy A., 35, dentist's assistant

🐾🐾🐾

I was in my first year at university. We'd met three weeks earlier when he came down from Glasgow to stay with a mutual friend. Now I was on my way to see him. Steve and I had been writing, and the first electric spark we felt on meeting seemed to be lasting. But now was the real test. Would it still be there when we met again?

I took the train at seven a.m., feeling apprehensive but extremely happy. The journey was a complicated one, but I'd been assured that the service was most reliable. This was true, at least until Bristol, then the trouble started.

First the driver collapsed and had to be taken away by ambulance. Then the engine broke down somewhere between Cheltenham and Gloucester. By the time we reached Birmingham, I'd missed the last connection to Glasgow.

Fortunately, we were told, the last train from York would be delayed for those who needed connections to Scotland. Unfortunately, on the other hand, obviously my arranged-with-great-foresight seat reservation was no longer mine. My small space of refuge was claimed by a commuter, who smirked unsympathetically at me over the lid of his laptop while I stood precariously amidst a crush of anxious travellers.

None more anxious than me.

With the help of a member of the train crew, I managed to obtain a courtesy phonecard with which to contact the ever-distant Steve. Our arrival was now estimated as ten p.m. rather than five p.m.

Naturally, nothing could be this simple. He was living in halls, and nobody wanted to answer the phone that day. I pictured Steve hanging round for hours, cursing, thinking 'Is this worth it?' . . .

Plan two: I phoned our mutual friend who could continue to try to contact him. The friend, of course, for once in his life, was at lectures. I had to leave a garbled message with his landlord's son. Garbled because the phonecard credits were moving much faster than the damn train.

We arrived at York a mere hour later than expected, and had to sprint from one end of the station to the other – up and down flights of steps, suitcase feeling as though I'd stuffed it with rocks, sweating, panting. The York driver was apparently a 'little impatient' by now. But at least, finally, I had a seat. The train, however, turned out to have no phone.

A fellow passenger, staggeringly more composed than myself, bent her ear to my plight and offered consolation in the form of a stiff vodka and orange. May she live a long and happy life. Feeling much better after this, I went to the train loo to change. It's hard squeezing yourself into a space the size of a phone box and trying not to touch any suspicious-looking stains. Anyway, I managed to don a rather elegant red dress which I had bought at great expense, hoping it might be just the trick to get the weekend off to a very good start.

My confidant alighted at Edinburgh wishing me luck, and I now sat alone on the nearly deserted train – apart from the usual mounds of debris: rolling Coke tins on the floor, the screwed-up wrappers. The buffet had closed, I was starving, the heating seemed to have gone off – and so, I fretted, might my romance. I mean, what a beginning.

Only forty minutes to go! A final – unexplained, naturally – delay of a paltry thirty minutes went almost unnoticed. I stepped out onto the deserted platform and searched the emptiness for signs of life. Possibly an ambulance, to cart off my exhausted, frozen body; but preferably, in the shape of Steve.

He wasn't there. After all I'd been through, he hadn't turned up.

I made my way to the nearest phone, obscenities streaming through clenched teeth.

Suddenly, a familiar voice called my name:

'Rachel! I saw this gorgeous woman in a red dress, but I didn't realize it was you!'

Well, thanks, Steve. Great to see you too.

(But, with the help of calming Yogic exercises, two years later I'm still riding those trains . . .)

Rachel K., 20, student

❦❦❦

I'd liked this guy for ages. He was really a good laugh. I was overjoyed to have got a date with him. He was lovely to be with.

I was looking to buy a new car, and he helped me. He found a nice little one for me, and seeing as he chose it, I wanted it too.

I was used to driving, but I didn't have much experience really. Nevertheless, Frank said I could drive his car, a Cortina, and he'd drive my new one home.

Driving Frank's car made me feel so special. I felt he must really like me to let me use it. I was bursting with happiness – so much so that I didn't notice the parked cars.

All three of them.

I passed out and woke up in hospital. Luckily I was OK. But Frank's loved Cortina, which was only a year old, was a complete write-off – as were Frank and I.

Paula E., 32, department store assistant

❦❦❦

He'd offered to take me out for a picnic in the countryside. We sat down in the balmy green meadow, hidden by bushes from some horses grazing right at the other end. He arranged several knives and forks and two champagne glasses on a large tablecloth. He then produced a whole variety of carefully prepared delicacies, including raw oysters, and a lobster salad. It was almost dusk and unfortunately, as the summer evening drew in, so did the gnats. This spoilt the whole romantic ambience somewhat as he kept slapping himself and cursing.

We decided to move away from the bushes, picking up all the knives and forks, the champagne glasses, the oysters and the lobster salad, rearranging them all once again a little further away.

The next half-hour passed peacefully enough. Things were going well and we were happily on to our third glass of champagne. Suddenly, a surprise ambush – by four very excited horses. They had obvious plans for the lobster salad.

I grabbed the champagne, he grappled with his delicacies and we tried to shoo the horses away between us. They were very obstinate, however, and weren't intending to leave without even a whiff of a lettuce leaf. So he told me to make my escape whilst he distracted them with a couple of apples.

I ran for the stile on the other side of the bushes, giggling because the stile happened to be quite a high one, which caused me several problems as I am only 5 foot tall. By the time he came racing into sight with four keen horses in hot pursuit of him and his lobster salad, I had got myself completely stuck on top of the stile and could not move a muscle without spilling even more champagne. The next few moments were all a blur. He got the champagne, I got over the stile and the horses got the lobster salad.

We found ourselves in a field full of cows, which we

decided were harmless enough and certainly preferable to the horses. So we again arranged the tablecloth, the knives, forks, champagne glasses and what was left of the goodies, and settled ourselves to finish the feast.

We drained the champagne and things began to get a little cosy. It was almost as if we had our own little world, snogging together beneath the stars, the sea twinkling in the background. We started to make love for the first time. At the height of our passion, we heard a squishing sound. Whipping our heads up, we found ourselves surrounded by a large herd of cows gazing at us with tremendous, bovine, passion-killing interest.

A romantic day in the country. Great idea.

Helen G., 24, modern languages student

❧❧❧

He was in his twenties, and had been married only a few months when his wife decided to leave him. I was asked to accompany him on a blind date to try and cheer him up. He was cut up about the break-up of his marriage and, I was assured, he only wanted some company. I was twelve years older than him. But then, toyboys are quite fashionable, I found myself thinking. You never know . . .

I arranged for him to take me out one Saturday evening. When he arrived at my door, I was confronted with all I can describe as an 'oversized jacket' with a thin body inside.

We set off to find a quiet venue, but we ended up in a very busy bar. He went to get us some drinks, and out came his wallet from his jacket pocket along with (wait for it) a great lump of wedding confetti. The poor lad had obviously decided to impress me by wearing a suit, but unfortunately it just happened to be the one he got married in and it was now about three sizes too big. He was so embarrassed, poor thing.

When we finally got ourselves seated, I decided to make polite conversation. I asked if he had any brothers or sisters. He told me had got a brother who was a lot older than himself, but they did not look alike. I asked him the name of his brother, and I almost spat my drink all over him when he told me.

His brother was my (very serious) ex of eighteen years previously. It was my turn to be embarrassed now – he couldn't stop laughing. He told me the woman his brother married (the one we finished for) still forbids any mention of my name in their house. He was in fits of laughter at the thought of him and myself turning up at his dear brother's house, only for his sister-in-law to have a heart attack.

Well, he'd needed cheering up.

Rhona C., 44, clothes shop assistant

❧❧❧

I felt very flattered to be invited to a classy nightclub by the best-looking guy in the office. It had been ages since my last date. I was a single mum in those days with an impossible workload, stress and strain written indelibly in shadows and pucks on my face. Thrift shop outfits hung unevenly on my coathanger-skinny frame; my hairstyle had been, well, neglected. I just could not imagine why he'd chosen me when all my female colleagues were so perfectly pruned and groomed, calm and confident. It was a complete enigma.

Anyway, I made a supreme effort with my appearance and hired a babysitter. I darted around like a demented chimp until I had completed the necessary chores, walked the dog, bathed the kids, and straightened up the chaos that hit every room daily. I even found time to prepare a supper tray for the babysitter, who was looking a bit apprehensive as she sidled past the dog and sat gingerly down on the only hair-free cushion. I paid her quickly in advance, in case she changed her mind.

I endeavoured to appear calm and organized when my date arrived, if a little breathless. He looked amazing: tall and slender in a perfectly fitted grey suit. He spoke softly, with gentle deliberation. My arms and legs started to prickle with goose bumps, and as I walked alongside him to the waiting car I felt my knees buckle.

The nightclub was buzzing with chatter and loud music, the atmosphere electrified by flashing coloured lights. I felt trills of excitement as we made our way to the circular bar set on a revolving platform. Its rotating movement was hardly detectable but effective, providing the bar-hoggers with an all-round view of the dance floor.

I saw the platform step, but for some reason my brain

failed to deliver the signal to my foot. I was busy rummaging through my handbag, searching for my purse to show willing to pay my way – and I missed the step. Hurtling out of control, I knocked into my date, causing him to stagger in an effort to regain his balance; I sprawled headlong on to the dance floor. My gaping handbag overtook me, skidding across the polished surface, spewing out its contents before it came to a halt.

My handbag epitomized my manic lifestyle. The kids called it 'Mum's Tardis'. I still carried supplies for all eventualities and every possible emergency, a habit formed in their baby years which I hadn't yet broken.

I closed one eye and squinted with the other at the trail of intimately personal belongings, strewn over a wide area. Combs, brushes, make-up and old receipts littered the floor. There was a clink as a teaspoon hit a metal chair leg, a packet of cigarettes was flattened underfoot by a dancer, the shoulder-strap lay motionless like a dead snake and twenty Lil-lets rolled in as many directions, gliding with ease in their cellophane wrappers.

He was very kind, bought me a drink – God I needed one – then asked me for a dance. I tried to smile an assent as I feverishly stuffed the retrievable items back into the handbag which had, somehow, lost half its original capacity.

The next dance was a 'smooch'. I buried my burning face into his grey lapels, grateful for the diversion. I was suddenly aware of his nearness, wallowing in the almost forgotten pleasure of being held by a warm human being.

Then I spotted a stray Lil-let, exposed and uncollected. I steered my date towards the offending object in the hope of kicking it into a dim corner. Alas; it hit a dancer's heel and came spinning back again. My date gallantly tried to ignore the fact that he'd trodden on it.

I struggled through another hour, drinking far too much at a ridiculous speed. As I swayed about, nursing a sore knee and hiccuping badly, feeling completely mortified, he held my coat politely and I fell thankfully into it.

The journey home was silent except for my hiccups.

On Monday morning, back at the office, I avoided his glance and reverted to addressing him as 'Mr —'.

Carol M., 49, payroll controller

🍷🍷🍷

During a three-week course I was extremely attracted to the guy sitting next to me. We had a mild flirtation going which had not yet gone beyond a couple of lunch dates. On the final day of the course, Dan asked me if I would join him and some of his friends in the local pub for a farewell drink, as it was his last night in London before he flew back to his job overseas.

Readily I agreed, and so several hours and too many drinks later we found ourselves heading back to my place for a last night of passion.

On the tube journey we were so wrapped up in each other that it was easy to forget where we were. I was suddenly aware that the train had stopped and looked up to see that we had reached my stop. 'We're here!' I shouted, scrambling up from my seat and hurling myself through the train doors just as they were closing.

The doors snapped shut behind me, the train moved off and I saw Dan peering at me through the window as the train gathered speed and sped off into the night.

I stayed on the platform, waiting and hoping for him to appear on the train coming back – but it was the last I ever saw of him.

Fate sure played gooseberry that night.

Sarah J., 23, civil servant

❧❧❧

I had joined a local dating agency and received forty-one replies, five of them Petes. I met one of the forty-one, a giant of a man called John, a part-time bouncer. We'd met one Sunday lunchtime and he'd invited me to his house for a meal the following Friday evening.

But I got cold feet and rang John to cancel. He was upset and kept telephoning me, trying to persuade me to change my mind. When I arrived home from work on the Friday, the phone was ringing – John again. While I was speaking to him, there was a knock on my front door. I asked John to hold on and went to open the door. There on my doorstep stood a Mick Jagger lookalike holding an enormous bottle of wine.

He was one of the Petes I had replied to by letter, so he had my address. I told him he should not have called round, but he seemed to be speaking in French. I asked him to wait there as I was on the phone and I closed the door to. I returned (feeling guilty somehow) to end the phone conversation and say goodbye to John.

Going back to the stranger, I found he had come in and was sitting at my dining-room table – rotten drunk, smoking and slumped over my antique linen tablecloth.

He was muttering away unintelligibly, and proceeded to burn a hole in the cloth, drop his cigarette and singe the carpet, lunge backwards and snap the back off the old chair, finally lunging forwards to send my dried flowers flying off the table.

I couldn't understand a word he was saying; was he a madman as well as a drunk? Now he was sliding off what was left of the chair on to the floor.

I started to get worried and thought he could become a bit violent. So I didn't tell him to go, and I didn't encourage him with pleasant small talk either. Instead I leaned against the radiator and stared at him appalled, wondering what I should do. The front door was behind him (as it opens straight into the dining-room of my old cottage) so I couldn't take a chance on trying to get out.

Then the phone rang in the sitting-room – thank God for John's persistence. I whispered to him to come quickly.

It took John twenty minutes to arrive, and it really did seem like an eternity.

I anticipated a fight; curtains torn down, ornaments and everything on the Welsh dresser to be smashed.

But John took one look at slumped Pete, lifted one of his arms and it flopped straight back down. John said Pete was practically unconscious with the drink. He lifted Pete over his right shoulder as if he were just a Christmas tree, and carried him off – Pete now shouting, still unintelligibly – down the road towards the river.

Half an hour passed, no sign of Big John. Then looking up the road I saw him strolling calmly towards me. He had left Pete at the police station for his own good as he thought he could have fallen into the river or under a car.

So I said I'd be round for the meal at nine p.m.

I had to now, didn't I? And anyway, John was growing on me a bit . . .

Well, I had Pete's large bottle of vino to take and I got ready. Suddenly, as I was about to open the door, it occurred to me that Pete could be lurking, in revenge, in my front garden. I opened the door very very cautiously, and there, inches from my face, was – a man.

I screamed and dropped the wine and he screamed and dropped all his toilet rolls and bottles of disinfectant.

It was a door-to-door cleaning stuffs salesman, and I'd scared us both into next week.

I went to John's shaking, laughing, a bag of nerves.

After the spaghetti bol he asked me to go and look at his water bed. I said all the excitement was too much and I felt quite faint and went home.

Cathy R., 37, housewife / part-time student / part-time care assistant

217

❦❦❦

When Tony asked me out I was ecstatic. I'd fancied him for ages and couldn't believe my luck. But I was nervous about dating as I'd recently split up with a long-term boyfriend and as a result, was an absolute bag of nerves by the time he picked me up.

He took me off to a restaurant and ordered sweet white wine – something that I never drink. My stomach was further turned by the first course, crab, which after two mouthfuls I decided was off.

By this time, the combination of nerves, sweet wine, foul-tasting crab and heat was making me nauseous and all I could think of was going home.

But Tony insisted that we go to a nightclub with his friends. We had only been in the club five minutes when I felt an overwhelming desire for fresh air. I managed to stagger out to the car park with my divine date in hot pursuit. The last thing I remember was throwing up all over his trousers as I fainted . . .

Stephanie L., 28, press officer

❦❦❦

Phil was my flatmate's younger brother. One night when my flatmate was late back from college, we got talking and ended up immersed in conversation till the early hours. This seemed to be a good start, so when he phoned up later that week to ask me out, I willingly accepted.

I should have read the warning signs when I saw what he was wearing. Normally one for jeans and casual tops, he was wearing a hideous mismatched suit – a green jacket (covered in cat hairs) and brown trousers. He shook my hand with his rather clammy one and asked me what I wanted to do.

From the confident, self-assured bloke I was used to he had changed into a nervous wreck.

We went off to play pool, as I assumed that might lighten him up a bit. It was then he confided the reason he was nervous. His older brother (my darling flatmate) had gone to see him earlier to ask why he wasn't more nervous; this was a First Date, after all. By the time Phil got to me, he'd been petrified into thinking that the fate of nations was at stake.

I had a bottle of wine at home, so we decided to go back and open that. The conversation was finally beginning to get more relaxed when there was a knock on the door. It was my flatmate. He asked if he could speak to Phil, and they vanished downstairs.

When Phil returned he was back to the tongue-tied mess he'd been before.

We continued drinking the wine. Again there was a knock at the door. My flatmate.

Again, Phil returned a terrified man.

We resumed our conversation – and it was really starting to go well. Phil was about to kiss me when there was another knock on the door. This time when Phil returned, I asked him why his brother kept calling him out to talk. Was there some terrible family crisis or what was it?

After a few minutes, Phil confessed that between

them, he and my flatmate had decided that he needed a few tips on how to handle women. He'd been getting pep talks every half hour on What To Do Next.

As if this wasn't bad enough, when he eventually kissed me, he started to emit the loudest moans I've ever heard. Anyone would have thought I was ravaging the poor boy to within an inch of his life. And of course, once my flatmate thought I was corrupting his little brother, there came another knock on the door . . .

Lizzie P., 19, student

❦❦❦

When I placed a 'companions' ad in the local newspaper, Jeff was one of the first to reply. His letter said he was an accomplished actor, tall, young, handsome and very, very energetic. He enclosed a photograph – wow! . . . This man was drop-dead gorgeous, this man deserved a phone call. His rich dark voice melted my heart, we talked passionately for two hours before arranging to meet.

The evening of the date arrived. I had spent a hot and sweaty afternoon searching for the perfect dress, a glorious shade of deep blue, and earrings to match. I *had* to look my best.

I set off for the wine bar, nervous as hell. Checking my reflection at the traffic lights I realized, to my horror, that the stone from one of my new very expensive earrings was missing.

After a frantic scrabble on the car floor I found it. What could I do? I couldn't meet Mr Wonderful with one earring, or worse still, no earrings at all. The earrings *made* the dress.

In a flash of inspiration I pulled in to a garage in search of Blu-Tack. Alas, no Blu-Tack, but instead one tube of Super Glue and a faux orange air freshener (I needed the pin to pierce the glue). I sat in the car, still shaking with nerves, earring in pieces, trying to stick the bloody thing together.

Time ticked on. I squeezed the tube . . . nothing. I squeezed again . . . minute droplet. I squeezed once more . . . huge blob of glue shot out and disappeared into the murky blackness of the car interior.

Resigned to my fate I removed the other earring and decided to face my knight in shining armour with bare earlobes. If he was any good it wouldn't matter.

I eased the car out into the traffic. First gear fine, second gear OK. I then realised something was badly wrong. I wanted to remove my hand from the gearstick to the steering wheel but I couldn't. It took me a little time to realize what had happened.

My hand was superglued fast to the gearstick.

Even worse, I was approaching the wine bar and *he* was waiting outside. He was looking for me and the car which I'd previously described. I wanted to die! The traffic was so slow, he spotted the car and was looking quizzically in my direction.

The lorry in front ground to a halt and he started to walk over to my car. I was going hot and cold. What could I say? 'Hello Jeff, I'm Karen. By the way, I've stuck my hand to the gearstick' . . .

Mercifully, the traffic moved on. I accelerated away leaving a bewildered Jeff – the potential love of my life – standing on the pavement.

I had to drive to my mother's house in a straight line. Roundabouts and corners are no good when you can only steer with one hand. I beeped the horn until she came out. She poured hot soapy water on my hand, gearstick (and car floor carpet) until she could unscrew the gear knob. I spent the evening in casualty.

In the end: Jeff called much later that night. I explained that I'd felt unwell, although I don't think for the slightest moment he believed me. I did meet up with him a month or so later, but we really didn't hit it off in the way I'd imagined. Unfortunately he was a good deal older than he originally said and didn't look to me as attractive as his photograph. His accomplished acting career amounted to a few 'extras' roles on TV. However, we parted on a friendly basis and I did get a postcard, from his next job, at a holiday camp.

Karen F., 27, administrator

ϘϘϘ

We'd met at a party, and this was our first date. Since espying him across a crowded room, enough electricity had sparked between us to power a small town.

We walked into the Indian restaurant, thinking a curry couldn't make us any hotter than we were already. It was very upmarket – white linen tablecloths, elegant cutlery, flowers, white candles in tiny glass holders.

We ordered dinner. We ate what little we could, hardly able to swallow a red-hot mouthful for searing lust. Suddenly, he could wait no longer. He reached over the table to pull me to him for a passionate snog.

And I burnt my chin on the candle.

Rachel M., 27, TV researcher

10
'But hell can turn to heaven':
Happy endings

I was still emotionally vulnerable after the break up of a long-standing relationship, and really very much outside the social circuit. My friend Kath, obviously concerned about my social, romantic and sexual welfare, contacted me to see if I would be interested in a 'blind date' with Sean, along with herself and her husband Neil.

Although Kath had never met Sean, Neil and Sean worked together and had, apparently, struck up a good relationship. Kath managed to make Sean sound a facsimile of my ex with whom I was still obsessed. 'I'm an old flame of his – he's an old inferno of mine.' (I was hoping for an opportunity to introduce my ex with the only humorous one-liner I had ever created.)

I should have realized. Any friend of Neil's was bound to be a pillock. Neil was loud and chauvinistic, not to mention uncouth, unruly, unkempt and dishevelled. Not that I particularly wanted a couth, ruly, kempt, and hevelled date!

To cut a long story short, I apprehensively agreed to go. On that fateful Friday evening I spent the usual three hours getting ready, making myself look as close to Sharon Stone – with knickers – as I'm ever going to look.

We had all arranged to meet at eight o'clock at the local trendy wine bar. It was Kath I spotted first, replete with an embarrassed expression. As she approached me, she whispered, 'I'm so sorry' – just as I caught sight of the reason for her penitence.

One million 'Hail Marys' were definitely in order. Sean was as refined-looking as a French prop forward and had the easygoing charm of a water buffalo. I was to discover that he thought of himself as the bees' knees (perhaps that's why he kept droning on). My look of disdain and disappointment I had to replace with that rehearsed plastic smile, perfected through long hours as a child listening to the monologues of my two maiden aunts.

Introductions were made, and for the next two hours we were regaled with a collection of bawdy stories, rude jokes and the like which I thought had been left behind in the fourth year. His childish attention-seeking behaviour would have made Gazza blush. Even Neil, as insensitive a human being as ever drew breath, eventually sensed my discomfort. He realized Sean was way over the top.

At around ten-thirty I felt, even with four or five glasses of an excellent 1981 Gran Reserva Spanish red inside me, I was going off my *rioja*. The final straw was when he bragged how he had persuaded this gorgeous French woman to come back to his flat with the memorable line, 'I feel so close to you, I want to sleep together like brother and sister.' The woman, seemingly reassured by this innocent yet intimate proposition, agreed to sleep (in the original sense) with him. When the inevitable happened, and Sean jumped on top of her, Colette (yes, they really do exist) protested vehemently. 'I saught zis was to be like bruzzer and seester.' Sean: 'Have you never heard of incest?'

With that, I made some pathetic excuse about having to get back early as I needed to be up at the crack of dawn to pick up a friend at the airport. Sean offered to drive me home, but I politely declined. I positively raced out of that wine bar, relieved that possibly the most awful, longest, most uncomfortable night since the Greeks took Troy had come to an end.

You know, sometimes I wonder why I ever married him.

Maire O'D., 36, field trainer for a building society

 ❦❦❦

I'd really taken a shine to Joe. We'd met at a mutual friend's dinner party. A few days later, he rang to say he was having friends for dinner in a week's time, and would I like to come?

Would I!

All week, he kept ringing me up.

'Rachel, how do you make gravy?'

'Rache, what temperature should I cook chicken at?'

'Er, Rache, how do you turn the oven on?'

Bit weird.

On the day of the dinner, at about six p.m., the phone rang. A desperate voice. Could I meet him at seven, outside Sainsbury's? Hey, romantic, or what?

I met him in the Sainsbury's car park. He was white

as a sheet. His hair looked wild, as though he'd been combing it frantically with his fingers.

'It's no good, Rache. I did try. The remains are in the bin. It looks like I dropped our dinner into a volcano.'

'Oh well,' I said, comfortingly. 'Food for four, won't be too bad.'

'Um, not exactly. There's actually, er, ten of us in all. The others are coming at eight-thirty.'

WHAT?

We ran round that supermarket like it was an all-you-can-grab-in-a-minute contest. We shot out of the revolving doors with a trolley laden so high it was in imminent danger of avalanche.

Muggins, natch, had to cook it.

Bloody hell, I thought, wrestling with clingfilm-wrapped broccoli, first date of the sodding century, this is.

But I have to say, in that hot, steamy kitchen, we got a bit hot and steamy too.

We're still together to this day – and at last I've taught him to cook.

Rachel M., 27, TV researcher

జముఖ్కు

Tom had been in the same crowd as me for a while, so I already knew him pretty well. He was good-looking and great company, and a more deep-rooted attraction had been there for a few weeks.

When our group separated at the end of an evening, Tom would always single me out for a quick kiss goodbye – and if we were really sozzled, we would have a good old snog outside the taxi rank!

This had carried on for a while; I was quite happy being single and looked forward to my weekend flirtations with Tom, even if he was seeing someone else. And so I was surprised when after one of our more passionate kisses at the end of one night over Christmas, he asked if he could take me out – just me and him on our own. It surprised me even more that he was completely sober when he asked me. Well, I thought, what the hell! Why not? It was Christmas, after all, and I was confident that however things turned out we would always remain friends. What was there to lose?

Our 'date' was the next week. Tom knew me fairly well; he had seen me out with the crowd enough times in my most reeling and raucous, plastered and pub-crawling state. So I wanted to surprise him with something different. Besides, I thought to myself, it was still Christmas . . .

So, the big day arrived. I rooted out my foot-file and grated the soles of my feet raw in an effort to make them baby soft (and kissable!). I nearly clogged the razor up as I shaved my legs for the first time in ages. Toenails painted crimson, and lashings of luxurious body lotion and expensive perfume. And then, completely out of character, I slipped into a glamorous dress. Hair and make-up immaculate. Things in the 'getting ready' department had never gone better; I felt good, I liked myself a lot and I was confident that I would have a good time.

A good time? It was wild! We had such fun in the full exhilarating, crazy and frivolous sense of the word. We were in complete hysterics over my descriptions of my boss – an antiquated, moronic and pathetically regimental museum-piece. To top the lot, by the time we jumped into the taxi home I was still feeling pretty gorgeous. I had somehow managed to keep my lipstick on, my hair wasn't stuck down to my head and my mouth didn't taste like the inside of a sumo wrestler's jockstrap like it usually did at the end of a night's drinking. And so, when the taxi stopped outside Tom's house and the invitation was there, I had no qualms. In fact, I couldn't think of a better finale to the seasonal celebrations.

Well, it certainly was a night to top all nights, and I felt I had entered into the New Year with more than a bang . . .

Tom had mentioned that he had to pick his car up from the garage in the morning, and off he went making me promise to stay in bed until he came back. So, as soon as I heard the front door close I leapt out of bed and rushed into the en-suite bathroom. I suddenly noticed a few things that I hadn't done when in my euphoric state the night before. Tom didn't use Old Spice aftershave did he? And surely that tube of expensive under-eye anti-wrinkle cream wasn't his? And then as I tried to clean my teeth with my finger coated in toothpaste it dawned on me. Not only had we been romping at his parents' house, but in his parents' *bed*! I did vaguely recall him mentioning that he was staying at his parents' house temporarily, and that they were away in Scotland for the New Year.

Oh well, it wasn't important. I repaired myself as best I could, and then arranged myself as seductively as possible back on the bed. I positioned myself so that my stockings and suspenders (yes, so what?!!) were alluringly visible. As a finishing touch, I orchestrated the duvet in such a way that I hoped Tom would be tempted into finding out what was underneath when he came back.

I must have dozed off. I heard the front door slam a while later, but it seemed a long time before the bedroom door opened and then:

'Who the hell . . .?'

That was most definitely not the voice of my man. I sat bolt upright in Tom's parents' bed – suspenders, boobs and all – and suddenly realized with appalled horror that not only was I face to face with Tom's father, but he was also my dreary, sourfaced and very severe boss!!

Tom seemed to take forever to come back from the garage.

In the end, the whole escapade was a blessing in disguise. My embarrassment prompted me to find another job which turned out to be better paid and with more responsibility; and two years later Tom and I are still together – and, I'm happy to say, this time installed in our own abode!

Theresa K., 26, secretary

🐾🐾🐾

231

I had fancied Steve for ages; at the time we were both students and living in a hall of residence. Our mutual friends just looked on it as an infatuation and thought I'd grow out of it.

But one night, returning from the pub, Steve came to my room (quite drunk) and suggested the two of us go to the cinema the following evening.

Naturally, I spent the whole of the next day washing my hair, debating whether to go the whole hog and put on a face pack, carefully selecting an outfit, and of course spreading the good news among friends.

But tea-time came and I still hadn't seen Steve. When he finally appeared at dinner, I spent a lot of time sending coy glances in his direction, but without eliciting any sort of reaction from him; I think he was rather bemused by it all.

Finally, one of my friends (the tables seated twelve), presumably out of pity at this sad spectacle, asked Steve – clearly referring to me – 'So, what are you two going to see tonight?'

To my utter horror and embarrassment, Steve was completely mystified by this. It soon became painfully obvious that he had absolutely no recollection of the night before. As the table fell silent, some sort of realization must have dawned, and he attempted to salvage the situation. 'Oh, are we *all* going to the cinema? What's *everyone* want to see?'

Thus, to my complete chagrin, and, I must add, the considerable amusement of certain friends, the hottest date of the decade looked more like a school outing as we set off with our eight chaperons!

But the story doesn't end there. Realizing what had

happened (and maybe trusting his drunken instincts), Steve took me out – unaccompanied – the following evening, and three-and-a-half years on we're still together. Here's to the communal date!

Theresa D., 22, student

❦❦❦

I was in my first year at university. It was 1969, and I wanted nothing more than to be a real hippy. But if I wanted to be Yoko Ono, I needed a John Lennon. The most essential criterion for a boyfriend, therefore, was that he resembled John Lennon as closely as possible. Long hair was an absolute prerequisite; ideally he should also have round glasses and wear anything long, flowing and Indian. I hadn't yet had a real hippy boyfriend. My northern university was a bit short of genuine hippies who had been to San Francisco or followed the hippy trail to Kathmandu.

One evening I went to a disco in the University Union, and there was a guy who satisfied all my criteria. He wore Indian love beads around his neck and wrists, an embroidered kaftan, purple loon pants and thonged sandals. He carried a hessian bag containing joss sticks. He wore round glasses. Best of all, he had long, curly, shining black locks. When he asked me to dance – or wave our arms about together to Jefferson Airplane – I couldn't believe my luck.

I was incredibly proud of having got myself a genuine hippy, and I persuaded a friend to come with me on our date so that she could admire him. I was wearing my most intricately embroidered kaftan and was carrying a fringed bag. An Indian scarf was wrapped around my head. My hair was freshly henna-ed and I had applied my purple Biba eye make-up with care. My best pair of crushed velvet crimson loon pants and a liberal splash of patchouli completed the ensemble.

So there I was sitting in the Union bar listing my new boyfriend's hippy credentials. I could tell that my friend was going green with envy, particularly when I mentioned the width of his bell-bottomed loon pants and the number of mirrors on his kaftan. In the midst of my eulogy, we were approached by a skinhead in a suit. 'Who's that straight?' I whispered to my friend – 'straight' meaning 'very conventional', which was a terrible insult in those days. Suddenly, as he came closer, I realized with horror who he was.

My gorgeous hippy.

I went bright red and was mortified when he sat down next to me. 'What's happened to your hair?' I blurted out. He then explained that he had been to the hairdresser's, who was a friend of his, after work. He couldn't see a thing without his glasses, and had taken them off during the haircut. When his friend had started trimming his hair, he had dozed off. His friend the hairdresser was a bit of a practical joker, and hadn't been able to resist shaving his entire head.

The suit was explained by his job in a bank – he hadn't had time to get changed before coming out.

A *bank*.

Working in a bank and having short hair were fearful crimes amongst would-be flower children, and I am ashamed to admit that I thought of denying all knowledge of him and setting off with my friend to find a real hippy. When he went to the loo, I said to my friend that he really had looked like a hippy on the previous evening. 'Never mind,' she said, 'he's got a nice face,' and sniggered.

Luckily, I overcame my prejudices and found that under that decent, respectable exterior lurked a really nice bloke. Five years later, the length of his hair didn't matter, kaftans had gone out of fashion, and we got married.

Diana S., 38, teacher

🐾🐾🐾

I'd just jacked in a Jack the Lad who was running two other women and I was seeing a married man who was about to get a flat for me. I worked in an Indian restaurant and was due to be picked up by him at twelve forty-five a.m. when I'd finished my shift.

However, earlier that evening the most stunning sexy Indian walked in and I was immediately taken with him. My boss knew the Indian and me well, and saw that he too felt the same way about me. So as not to embarrass me, he spoke in Indian to him and somehow masterminded the whole thing. So I ended up leaving the restaurant early, thus avoiding the married man, and going off with my Indian 'prince'.

It was a magical night. Morning dawned to crashes on the door and my irate married man demanding to be let in. Well, if I'd have been my Indian – because I'd told him about the Jack the Lad and the married man – I'd have only thought of it as a one-night stand. So I hustled him into the bathroom with his clothes (not noticing his shoes left in the middle of the sitting-room floor), gave him the backdoor key, instructions to leave in fifteen minutes and keep quiet, and to ring me later if he wanted to.

I opened the door to my married man nonchalantly – 'Oh hi, how are you, are you ready to go and see the flat?' He was suspicious and coldly calm. Spotted the shoes and my red face and said he was busting and needed to use the loo. There was nothing else for it. 'Two's company in a bathroom. I think you'd better go.'

Embarrassment? I nearly died. But my Indian prince – well, we're still together six years on.

Becky L., 35, waitress

ఇఇఇ

An ex-colleague of mine who had joined the fire service introduced me to his boss at our local swimming club. His boss asked me out on a date, so we then arranged to meet on the Saturday. We went to the local funfair. I love funfairs, but unknown to me he hated them.

Not wanting to lose face, he agreed to go on the waltzers. We started spinning gently, but not for long – the waltzer car began to spin faster and faster. I looked at my date in time to see his mouth open in terror and his false teeth go flying across the car and on to the wooden boards. His secret was well and truly out and bounding across the floor.

As the ride stopped, he was out of the car in a flash on his hands and knees trying to retrieve both sets of teeth which were gaily bouncing in opposite directions; his 'macho firefighter' image shattered. The crowds of people getting off and on the waltzer cars were laughing and giggling as they tried to avoid the errant molars. Grabbing his teeth, he turned and looked at me, hoping I hadn't noticed. But I'm ashamed to admit that I was helpless with laughter, holding my sides and tears rolling down my cheeks. He had to buy a tin of cola in order to rinse his teeth, as there was no water, then replace them in a very sorry mouth.

When he asked me out again I had to say yes just to see if anything else would happen.

Which it did, often.

Once we went swimming on a Sunday afternoon. The pool was crowded, so at one stage we lost sight of each other. I stood up in the shallow end to look for him and there he was at the deep end, climbing out and sitting on the edge with heels in the overflow gutter.

Being a man he sat with his legs at a quarter to three – but unaware that the stitching on his Bermuda-style swimming trunks had come undone. His trunks now took on the appearance of a mini skirt, revealing another well-kept secret. I frantically tried to swim to him, signalling and shouting. It's amazing just how far a length is when you're in a hurry. Unfortunately, a very elderly female attendant noticed. The last thing I saw was my very red-faced man being escorted to the changing rooms by the attendant, who was busily shouting 'Pervert' very loudly so everyone could hear.

All of this happened a long time ago. He is now a 'macho' policeman and we have been married for fifteen years and have two wonderful children. I love him more now than I did on our wedding day. Which also turned into a bit of a disaster . . .

Wendy E., 38, part-time nurse

❧❧❧

I was working as the personal assistant to the managing director of a major company. One day in September 1990, something came over me in a wave. I asked a very senior (in position, not age) – and single! – executive of the company if he would like to come out on a date. I had never even had a conversation with him.

Much to my surprise he said yes.

Ten days later he collected me from my home and took me to a very sophisticated restaurant by the river. We were seated right in the middle of the restaurant with all spotlights directed on us. We ordered, had our first course and then the waitress brought over two tall glasses of what looked like ice cream. I raised my hand and in an extremely loud, confident voice told her (and the whole packed restaurant), 'You must have the wrong table, we haven't had our main course yet.'

The waitress looked at me with contempt, and my date explained to me very quietly that it was sorbet and was meant to cleanse my palate before the main course. I was so humiliated I wanted the ground to open up and take me a million miles away.

Needless to say I never thought I would see him again.

But I did, and the next date we both just roared with laughter about it. Almost a year to the day we married, and two years later have just had a baby daughter!

Nikki S., 34, personal assistant

♔♔♔

I stood within the frame of my front door, a picture of sheer elegance and class. A shimmering, clinging evening dress, long dark curls falling onto and beyond my shoulders. There before me, a tall, blonde, blue-eyed man in full evening dress.

He beamed with delight, his own smile as broad as mine. God, I felt good, and boy, did he look good. This was my kind of date. A stunning man and the sort of ball you only see on the television, usually with the Queen in attendance.

Matt escorted me to his car, a battered old Volvo. It wasn't exactly what I'd had in mind. But you could tell he'd washed, waxed and hoovered it, and myself and my dress appreciated his efforts.

We got to the venue half an hour later, and parked between a Rover and a Calibra. Matt looked embarrassed. 'You should have come in one of those,' he said, looking longingly at the Rover. 'I prefer the driver of the Volvo,' I said, trying to sound supportive.

We crunched our way over the gravel from the car park (me on tiptoes so as not to scratch the heels of my new shoes) and arrived at the biggest door I've ever stood in front of. It opened before Matt even had a chance to ring the bell. 'Good evening sir, madam.'

I entered the ballroom, took a deep breath and held it, making sure I looked as slim as possible. I wanted Matt to feel proud. I wanted his friends to look at me and say, 'Is she with him?' I took another few steps.

And then it happened.

On my next step, the stiletto heel of my shoe sunk into a crack in the highly polished wooden floor. I was catapulted out of my shoes, hopping stupidly into the waiter in front of me who, together with his tray of champagne glasses, crashed to the floor. I fell with him, or should I say on top of him. Just as I tensed my body for the landing, I heard it.

Oh hell. A rip, a tear, and there for all the world to see were my cheeks. If they could, they would have blushed.

It was at that moment that I became eternally grateful for my G-string. At least it helped me retain some of my dignity with a thousand pairs of eyes glued to my bottom.

After what seemed like an eternity, people came forward to help. The waiter, unhurt, offered me his jacket. It was just long enough to hide my embarrassment. I knew Matt was at my side, but I could not look at him.

'My shoe,' I whispered, 'could you get me my shoe.' The waiter, totally unruffled by his tumble, obliged. I limped behind him, first 5ft 11in then 5ft 8in, 5ft 11in, 5ft 8in. I was not taking off the other shoe. I still had some pride even if half of that was wedged solid into the floor.

It wouldn't move. The waiter got down on all fours and pulled, twisted, tugged and yanked, until it finally gave way. The heel, however, didn't. It remained in the floor, laughing at me.

I took what was left of my pride and headed for the door.

Matt took hold of my arm, now I could no longer avoid him. I took a deep breath and looked into his eyes. He was smiling, a big Cheshire cheesy smile. 'Madam can't possibly walk to the car over the gravel now, can she? Allow me.' He picked me up and carried me back to his now very appealing Volvo. He helped me in and then got in himself. He looked at me and smiled, then laughed, then I laughed; and we both collapsed into uncontrollable hysterics.

We were still laughing when we got a puncture on the way home. Matt got covered in dirt, and tore his shirt – but it was the funniest flat I've ever had.

My mum opened the door, her initial horror turning into a big grin. 'No need to ask if you had a nice time then.' Her daughter and date had left looking like a couple from an episode of *Dallas*; she had returned with a ripped dress, a waiter's jacket, a broken shoe, and a slashed and oil-streaked boyfriend.

I still laugh, five years later, but cringe with embarrassment too.

As for Matt, well, I had to marry him. I had to make sure he never told anyone! But at least hell can turn to heaven, after all.

Louise R., 29, car rental agent

Have *you* had a Date from Hell?
Or a Holiday from Hell?
Or suffered under a Boss from Hell?

If so, write and tell us about it!

The funniest stories will be published in future books. Length: no more than 750 words – typed if possible.

Send your letters asap to Maryon Tysoe, c/o Headline, 338 Euston Road, London NW1 3BH. Please state your age and occupation.

Headline Book Publishing reserves the right to edit letters for publication and to use them for publicity surrounding the book. All names will be changed.

Sexual Awareness

Enhancing Sexual Pleasure

Barry and Emily McCarthy

ILLUSTRATED   NEW UNEXPURGATED EDITION

This book is written to show individuals and couples how to enhance their sexual pleasure. It is focused on feelings and fulfilment, and emphasizes a joyful expression of sexuality and intimacy.

The path to a new awareness includes chapters on:
The Pleasure of Touching
Self-Exploration
Increasing Arousal For Women
Becoming Orgasmic
Learning Control
Overcoming Inhibition

With the current emphasis on the importance of just one sexual partner, this is a timely publication designed to show you just how to make the most of that relationship, and how to build a new sexual partnership.

NON-FICTION/REFERENCE   0 7472 3561 9

More Non-Fiction from Headline:

GRUB ON A GRANT

CAS CLARKE

Cheap and Foolproof Recipes for All Students

'...a useful little book for an absolute beginner. My children simply loved her Varsity Pie.' Prue Leith, *Guardian*

'...written by a student who experienced the problems of cooking for herself for the first time while at the University of Sussex; she reckons her recipes are foolproof, and so they are.' *Daily Telegraph*

'...full of extremely practical and sensible advice and some hilarious cartoons, giving an exciting repertoire of meals whatever the culinary abilities.' Jill Probert, *Liverpool Daily Post*

Grub on a Grant found an unexpectedly large and eager market when it was first published in autumn 1985. Perhaps it struck a special chord with young people because it recognized that they are short not only of money but of time and culinary gadgetry as well - but they do like to eat well, and they especially love food with clearly identifiable flavours. For this revised and updated edition of her book Cas Clarke has greatly expanded the vegetarian section. There are also some exciting dinner party recipes and a chapter on slow cooking.

Whether you are on a student grant, unemployed or just generally impoverished, you'll find this new edition of *Grub on a Grant* a very sound investment.

NON-FICTION/COOKERY 0 7472 3560 0

JOHN PARKER

THE LAST GREAT LOVER OF HOLLYWOOD

Warren Beatty is a movie star of the sort they don't make any more. He is famous for being famous. He is famous for going to bed with the famous. His sexual liaisons have brought him more publicity than his movies and his list of conquests includes up-to-the-minute stars like Madonna and Annette Bening who finally coaxed Beatty into marriage and fatherhood.

But behind the playboy façade Beatty has created his own image of an elusive, narcissistic intellectual, a reluctant star, embroiled in politics. As producer of the wildly successful *Bonnie and Clyde* he became a multi-millionaire before he was thirty and has never had to accept work that did not appeal to him.

Actor, writer, director, producer, he has become one of the most powerful men in Hollywood. With the help of frank reminiscences from friends and associates, bestselling author John Parker has written a riveting and richly colourful portrait of one of Hollywood's most compelling, enigmatic stars.

'John Parker's *Warren Beatty* is as slick as its subject... There is masses of showbiz gossip. A good racy read.' *The Times*

NON-FICTION/BIOGRAPHY   0 7472 4063 9

A selection of non-fiction from Headline

THE DRACULA SYNDROME	Richard Monaco & William Burt	£5.99 ☐
DEADLY JEALOUSY	Martin Fido	£5.99 ☐
WHITE COLLAR KILLERS	Frank Jones	£4.99 ☐
THE MURDER YEARBOOK 1994	Brian Lane	£5.99 ☐
THE PLAYFAIR CRICKET ANNUAL	Bill Frindall	£3.99 ☐
ROD STEWART	Stafford Hildred & Tim Ewbank	£5.99 ☐
THE JACK THE RIPPER A–Z	Paul Begg, Martin Fido & Keith Skinner	£7.99 ☐
THE *DAILY EXPRESS* HOW TO WIN ON THE HORSES	Danny Hall	£4.99 ☐
COUPLE SEXUAL AWARENESS	Barry & Emily McCarthy	£5.99 ☐
GRAPEVINE: THE COMPLETE WINEBUYERS HANDBOOK	Anthony Rose & Tim Atkins	£5.99 ☐
ROBERT LOUIS STEVENSON: DREAMS OF EXILE	Ian Bell	£7.99 ☐

All Headline books are available at your local bookshop or newsagent, or can be ordered direct from the publisher. Just tick the titles you want and fill in the form below. Prices and availability subject to change without notice.

Headline Book Publishing, Cash Sales Department, Bookpoint, 39 Milton Park, Abingdon, OXON, OX14 4TD, UK. If you have a credit card you may order by telephone – 0235 400400.

Please enclose a cheque or postal order made payable to Bookpoint Ltd to the value of the cover price and allow the following for postage and packing:
UK & BFPO: £1.00 for the first book, 50p for the second book and 30p for each additional book ordered up to a maximum charge of £3.00.
OVERSEAS & EIRE: £2.00 for the first book, £1.00 for the second book and 50p for each additional book.

Name ....

Address ....

....

....

If you would prefer to pay by credit card, please complete:
Please debit my Visa/Access/Diner's Card/American Express (delete as applicable) card no:

Signature .... Expiry Date ....